UNIVERSAL
an
NUMEROLOGY

C000071937

DESTINY of **9** HUMANKIND

A UNIFYING SYNTHESIS for the KEY NUMBERS of

The HOLY BIBLE
The GREAT PYRAMID
The MAYAN CALENDAR
The FATIMA PROPHECY
The EVOLUTION of AMERICA
The PYTHAGOREAN DIVINE TRIANGLE
NUMEROLOGY and ASTROLOGY in WORLD
ECONOMICS
and
EXTRATERRESTRIAL and COSMIC CONNECTIONS

WILLIAM P. MAYNARD

Ask, and you will receive; seek, and you will find;
knock, and it will be opened.

Jesus/Jeshua of Nazareth
(the metaphysical Christ)

This book is dedicated to all those truth-seeking entities specifically mentioned in these chapters who generously have imparted their acquired knowledge so that the primarily material-oriented segment of humankind may be inspired and motivated to enter the spiritual pathway toward a higher consciousness and eventual Enlightenment.

This book is especially dedicated to the Christ Soul and its many specific incarnations, but specifically to the most recent lifetime as Jesus/Jeshua of Nazareth and His special mission of presenting a New Covenant to our unique Adamic race.

CONTENTS

INTRODUCTION

On January 3, 1976, my normal, comfortable, uneventful material world was turned upside down when I casually opened a small paperback book that my wife had brought home from the local library. The book was entitled, Edgar Cayce: The Sleeping Prophet, and she had brought this book home numerous times before and suggested that I read it. However, I was too busy with my demanding, detailed aerospace work in San Diego to respond to a superficial distraction that I really wasn't interested in anyway. But on this particular Saturday afternoon I had just finished building a 25-inch Heathkit color television set, as well as my income tax return, so I rather unconsciously picked up the book that she had left conspicuously on the kitchen countertop. I happened to open the book to the chapter on incurable diseases and became engrossed in the text because since a child I had been very interested in medical research, which I now realize could be attributed to my Pisces Sun Sign, which is quite augmented by my Scorpio Ascendant/Rising Sign.

My concentration on the material world at that time precluded any interest or consideration of such esoteric topics as reincarnation and karma, but in retrospect it was all during the previous year that I had become interested in the paranormal realm or dimension. Yet, if I had opened that book to the chapter dealing with prophecies, I am certain that I would have thrown the book down in disgust because at that time I had manifested an intense dislike and disdain for "soothsayers" because I felt that they were charlatans only interested in personal material gain and ego inflation. However, the information concerning incurable diseases and health in general captivated me to the point where I was able to digest the rest of the book, which induced me to contact the Edgar Cayce Foundation and its Association for Research and Enlightenment in Virginia. I soon initiated membership therein, while also learning of their international network of Search for God Study Groups. Much to my amazement and delight, I discovered that there was a Group less than one mile from my residence.

Having joined the spiritually-oriented study group and learned to meditate properly, on the third month, near my birthday of March 3rd, I awakened at about 6 a.m. and experienced a vision (like viewing a live stage play) in which Jesus of Nazareth was praying in the garden at Gesthemane. The scene then shifted to Jesus on the cross of crucifixion, and I heard Him say, "Father, forgive them, for they know not what they do." Immediately, what I only can describe as a powerful electrovibrational sensation began to develop in my hands and I presumed that I was being given the power for magnetic healing (laying-on-of-hands, colloquially). The phenomenon continued up my arms, down through my chest, then stopped at my waist, which urged me to utter aloud, imploring Christ, "Please don't stop; go all the way!" Then the vibrational energy proceeded all the way to my feet, and I just lay there, purging, because by now I felt I was undergoing a *cleansing* process for some reason.

Soon, I began hyperventilating (as I later diagnosed my reaction), and it seemed that the phenomenon continued unabated for about ten minutes before subsiding, upon which time I felt completely exhausted from this whole mystical encounter with the Christ Spirit, which I now refer to as my "Road-to-Damascus" experience, similar to the traumatic Christ Spirit encounter that dramatically changed Saul to the apostle Paul. I should further note that this same electrovibrational energy would manifest at about six o'clock each morning three months later as I attended my first week-long A.R.E. conference in northern California that was entitled, "Jesus, the Essenes, and the Second Coming."

After about a year of concentrated study of the thousands of Edgar Cayce spiritual "readings" that emanated from his larynx while he was in a self-induced altered state of consciousness, I obviously was somehow directed to a reading that stated, "All those, then, that were cleansed by Him have been called—*are* called—for special missions, for activities in each experience in and among men, that they, as souls, as portions of the life, as portions of the whole, may demonstrate, may give, the blessings to many." (Excerpt of Cayce Reading 295-8) Hopefully, the spiritual and metaphysical contents of this book will inspire and motivate any reader to diligently seek for Truth, albeit I still am trying to interest the medical establishment about the Xenon Technology for general healing and regeneration of the human body, and possibly also to raise the consciousness of humankind in this crucial period of our spiritual evolution, as vividly depicted in Matthew 24 of the Holy Bible.

To further validate and elucidate the meaning of my mystical experience with the Christ Spirit, in March, 1982, I was offered an opportunity to obtain a soul-life reading from a scientifically-tested trance medium. Since I was still struggling on the spiritual pathway toward Enlightenment, I succumbed to the temptation regarding a possible shortcut in the arduous process. But first, I felt the need to apply the proper preparation for such a serious matter, as directed in the Cayce spiritual advice, so I prayed and meditated at 2 a.m. for three consecutive nights, hopefully to engender and receive the greatest accuracy and validity for the past-life reading.

During the soul-life reading, the voice cautioned me against using dreams "as a material concern", so I knew the information would be accurate because I had been utilizing intentionally-manifested dreams to purchase industrial stocks for monetary gain, which proved to be quite successful. The rest of the reading was unchastising and referred to my interest and association with John the Baptist, who the source of the reading described as "the forerunner of the Spiritual Illumination of Life", which is a perfect description of Jesus/Jeshua the Christ. The source revealed that I had been a member of the judicial Sanhedrin Council in Jerusalem, and later witnessed the execution of Jesus of Nazareth. The aforementioned cleansing process that I experienced indicates that I had been involved with the legal aspects of this execution at Calvary/Golgotha, however misguided I may have been in this matter that the chief priest, Caiaphas, had pursued so vigorously, and adamantly demanded a death verdict from the Council.

To substantiate this supposition, all my life, that is until my soul-life reading in 1982, I had had a half-inch diameter round, reddish-brown spot at the same location on the top of both feet. During the Easter period that occurred soon after my past-life reading in March, both round spots became bright red, and I quickly surmised and understood that they were two benign stigmata that signified the nail holes in Christ's feet at Calvary. Soon, both disks disappeared, and they never have returned during all these succeeding years of my life.

As a final, seemingly-corroborating factor, I should relate the feline phase of my subsequent life experiences in this incarnation. Apparently, the traumatic effect that had manifested as I witnessed the wrongful Crucifixion had such an impact on me that, much like the Christian-persecuting Saul, I quickly became a convert and began a teaching mission because my soul-life reading also revealed that my son and I had been spiritual teachers in Rome and Athens. The source of the reading added that I had been executed in the Coliseum in Rome by Tiberius because of my "refusal to give up the spiritual pathway", and probably also because of my attempts to save Christians from execution in the arena during my "talks with Tiberius." (Incidentally, my son, David, who is a fine artist, like Andrew Wyeth, drew a detailed ink-drawing of the Coliseum when he was seventeen years of age, and he still does not remember why he had chosen to do it at that time in his young life. Coincidentally, and even synchronistically, this was at almost the same time when I had experienced my mystical encounter with the Christ Spirit.)

Like my wife, I had always been very fond of cats and even took them to bed with me as a child, even sneaking the cat in through the bedroom window. Soon after reading the Cayce book in California, a stray, tan-colored cat that looked like a female lion came to our house and wouldn't leave, so we adopted it. However, every time I would stroke its fur my whole body would begin to itch intolerably. During these many succeeding years, two more tan-colored, lion-like cats have found their way to our home after the previous cat had died, the third and last having departed in 2006. Could these three cats have represented—or even have been—the lions that killed me in the arena in Rome? Unlike the severe allergic reactions I had experienced with the three lion-like cats, I can pet other types of cats without suffering adverse effects. To support this past-life scenario, the Edgar Cayce spiritual source once told a woman who had received a soul-life reading that her present dog had been her pet lion during a previous incarnation in Rome. Also, the Cayce source indicated that some allergies that manifest during the current lifetime have their roots in traumatic past-life experiences, especially those that had resulted in the death of the physical body.

While I still was participating in the weekly meetings of our Search for God Study Group in San Diego, one of the members introduced me to the Texas-based Association for the Understanding of Man (AUM), and I soon initiated membership therein because the metaphysical information that had been emanating from trance medium (like Edgar Cayce) Ray Stanford, their psychic facilitator, confirmed the very enlightening

Cayce information, but even transcended and expanded on it all, especially regarding the Mayan calendar/Tzolkin, the Pythagorean Divine Triangle (Life Theorem) and the Fatima Prophecy, all of which are thoroughly discussed and evaluated in this book.

Within the first year of my membership in the A.R.E., it must have been spiritual forces or intuition that introduced me to numerology, and I was soon fascinated with the numbers of this primary spiritual science. Since the numbers appeared to be so meaningful and valid in my own life, I soon began to create natal numeroscopes that seemed to really help people to understand themselves and their purpose in this lifetime. I later complemented the numbers with astrology because it became evident that most entities (spirit, mind and body) are struggling with their complex personalities and fail to recognize that the numbers pertain primarily to the soul and its mission in any lifetime, whereas the astrological indicators apply primarily to the basically-triangular personality that terminates when the soul returns to the etheric spirit realm.

In the third—3 is the *whole* number—phase of my spiritual transformation, a professional numerologist friend sent me a book in 1980 that was entitled, The Book of Knowledge: The Keys of Enoch, which I wouldn't read for a long time because the "Keys of Enoch" term gave me the impression that this book had been written by a spiritual seeker who may have been seduced by the "lunatic fringe" aspects of metaphysics and religion in general, which include a generous portion of ignorance and form. However, out of respect for and obligation to my friend, I began to read—no, *study*—the amazing contents of the book that I found quite difficult to understand at that time of my spiritual evolution. And yet, I engendered a strong feeling that the contents were valid and presented a comprehensive depiction of who humans really are, why we are here in this three-dimensional earth plane, and also where we are destined to go when we complete the ordeal of Soul Perfection as a result of our successful spiritual evolutionary process. How long a person lives is really unimportant. What truly matters most is what you do while residing as an entity in the earth plane.

In retrospect, I now can understand and assimilate the reason why it was necessary for me to experience the Edgar Cayce (A.R.E.) vast source of metaphysical knowledge, the expanded Ray Stanford (A.U.M.) information and the culminating, profound spiritual and cosmological information in The Book of Knowledge: The Keys of Enoch that was presented to Dr. (two Ph.D.s) James J. Hurtak from a seemingly very spiritual source while he was meditating and praying concerning his strong desire to help his fellow human beings, and his Academy for Future Science is perpetuating his purpose of providing enlightenment to humankind. It should be no real surprise that the central focus and common denominator for all three of these unique sources of spiritual information and guidance are Jesus/ Jeshua the Christ and the Holy Trinity in general, and they, with the numbers, comprise the Unifying Synthesis of the mysteries that are presented and examined in this book.

FOREWORD

This book is intended to function as a unifying synthesis concerning some of the most prominent and perplexing mysteries of this world and its neighbor planets in this solar system, and even other celestial and cosmic conditions that affect humankind in some way. When we discover that the true architect/designer of the Great Pyramid in Egypt was one of the physical incarnations of the Christ Soul and that Quetzalcoatl/Kukulkan/Viracocha (Aztec, Maya, Inca deities, respectively) were all names that were applied to the Christ disciple, Didymos Thomas (the so-called "White God in the Americas"), then we can engender a more serious attitude toward and a deeper study of these mysteries, and especially concerning the critical, imminent year of 2012 that is the culmination of the chronology of the Mayan Sacred Calendar (Tzolkin), according to various interpreters and meticulous scientific researchers.

Humankind has been so long involved in and restricted to the *material* and *physical* sciences that it relatively or virtually has ignored the third (3 is the *whole* number), and arguably the most important, spiritual science of *metaphysics*, which permits any entity (a human being comprised of the three essential components of spirit, mind and body) to enter into and experience the *real* domain and dimension of Spirit.

Perhaps the most useful aspects of the vast realm of metaphysics are the spiritual sciences of numerology and astrology. However, whereas astrology appears to primarily pertain to the human personality and its associated behavior and activities while existing in the material earth plane, the numbers seem to primarily pertain to the soul, beginning with the numbers/digits of each individual's birth date that reveal the basic purpose and mission of the entity in any incarnation or sojourn in Schoolhouse Earth. Secondly, the letters of the birth name, when converted to numbers, reveal any specific karmic lesson(s) that must be addressed and dissipated in this lifetime, and these birth name numbers also indicate the type of mental and physical activities that will be needed to successfully accomplish the soul's mission in this incarnation. Unfortunately, since many human beings of our present Adamic race have been assigned—and actually accepted—very complex, dichotomous and conflicting personalities, they spend much of their precious life just struggling to understand their personality traits, never realizing their true identity at the *soul* level and its unique purpose for having entered physical embodiment from its natural etheric spiritual realm. As the Holy Bible and the Edgar Cayce spiritual source urgently advise, the great study of humankind should be Self, and numerology and astrology appear to be the simplest and most effective mediums for accomplishing this formidable task. A channeled spiritual source said that "remarkable intuitions" can manifest in the mind via the study and application of numerology and astrology as a "media of intuition."

Regarding this mandatory spiritual evolutionary process that is strongly associated with the number 9, the Christ Soul, when teaching in the earth plane as Jesus/Jeshua of Nazareth, emphasized the importance of this soul evolutionary process when He advised and urged, "Be perfect, as your Father in heaven is Perfect!" Since this idyllic state of soul perfection cannot possibly be attained in merely one life cycle, we need to realize and acknowledge that many lifetimes should be necessary to accomplish Soul Perfection. Since our dualistic condition can result in both positive and negative karma and the sins of both commission and omission, this involves the immutable law of cause-and-effect, meaning that we truly reap what we sow, even if it is postponed until a future physical incarnation. Instead of the trivializing, proverbial "chicken-or-the-egg" philosophy, we need to ask, "Which came first, the adult human being or the baby human being?" Indeed, without the concept and reality of reincarnation and karma, a human biological, physical existence and lifespan truly could not, and does not, make much sense.

The numbers 3, 6 and 9 (which is the important triplication of the 3 and is the human destiny number) and the succeeding numbers, 18 and 27 (which is the triplication of the crucial number 9) appear to be the most prevalent and pervasive in the affairs of humankind, as the chapters of this book will conspicuously illustrate. However, the anomalous, inconsistent number 17 also is pervasive and omnipresent in the affairs of humankind, but generally as a purging vibratory energy that pertains both to *suffering* and *redemption*, as depicted in the very first book (Genesis) of the Holy Bible wherein the human-eradicating Flood began on the seventeenth (17) day of a month. However, Noah's great ark, after a long ordeal (symbolized by the number 17), grounded on a mountain also on the seventeenth (17) day of a month. This also is the key number in the message of the Great Pyramid (a "Bible in stone"), the Pythagorean Divine Triangle (Life Theorem), and even concerning the birth and evolution of the United States of America. It is presented only indirectly in the New Testament's Gospel of John concerning the symbolism of the 153 (=9) fish that Christ either materialized or directed into the empty fishnet of the disciples, an incident that has perplexed theologians and Bible scholars perhaps for many centuries. This book attempts to offer a plausible and very meaningful solution, via the number 17, to this seemingly enigmatic act by Christ just prior to His final Ascension at this third (3) and last appearance to the disciples following His crucifixion. Indeed, the number 17 is a key number associated with the ("dwarf") planet, Pluto, that represents the transformation of human consciousness, according to both astrology and the Edgar Cayce psychic source of spiritual philosophy.

Humankind has experienced three (3) evolutionary revolutions, viz., agricultural, industrial and the present intensifying communications revolution. Since the concept of the Holy Trinity obviously emphasizes that the number 3 is the *whole* number in life, then it would appear that this current communications revolution should be the last of these cycles in the history of humankind. Hence, the year 2012 that seems to be permeating the consciousness of many people in the world now may prove to be accurate regarding a final "metamorphosis" of the species Homo sapiens, such as the scenario described by Jesus/Jeshua in Matthew 24 that many Christians refer to as the *rapture*. Even the spiritual sciences of numerology and astrology are confirming this traumatic, climactic scenario.

The Edgar Cayce spiritual source stated that the best description of God is *electricity*, which is the basic nature of the cosmos. Regarding the dimension of Spirit (the "other side"), the Cayce source described it to be very much like a "dream." Continuing with this spiritual philosophy and reality, the Cayce spiritual source also stated that the strongest force in man is *sex* and that *fear* is the most destructive force in man. But perhaps the most succinct and obviously the most important revelation that emanated from the Cayce spiritual source pertained to the primary reason why each "entity" must experience repeated "sojourns" in Earth's three-dimensional plane. It simply, but emphatically, stated that each entity is here to "meet Self!" Interpretation: Absolutely no one can avoid or circumvent the immutable spiritual law of cause-and-effect (karma).

Instead of merely being a unifying synthesis for the significant numbers of all the subjects and information contained and discussed in this book, the reader eventually will come to realize that all of these numbers are essentially merely only a symbolic expression of the *real* Unifying Synthesis: the Christ Soul!

This author fervently desired to publish this book with the relatively simple title, Toward a Number 9 Consciousness, but the selected existing title really was required to indicate the magnitude and scope of the influence and meaning of the simple language of numbers and how this basic number 9 has been applied by Spirit to indicate even the *destiny* of humankind. Considering the present appalling global sociological and spiritual conditions, humankind truly needs desperately to manifest a number 9 Consciousness.

CHAPTER 1

The Meanings of the Nine Basic Numbers of the Spiritual Science of Numerology

Based on the twenty-six letters of the English alphabet, the numbers are assigned to the letters as shown in the following table, and the value of the letters has evolved from the Pythagorean numerical system, as depicted in philosopher Manly P. Hall's masterful, comprehensive, voluminous work entitled, The Secret Teachings of All Ages.

1	2	3	4	5	6	7	8	9
A	B	C	D	E	F	G	H	I
J	K	L	M	N	O	P	Q	R
S	T	U	V	W	X	Y	Z	

Please notice that there are only two letters to accommodate the important number 9, which pertains to compassion, understanding and humanitarianism. Thus, each person's birth name has only two opportunities for receiving a number 9 versus three chances for all the other letters. And yet, very few people have the number 9 missing from their birth name as it appears on the birth certificate, regardless of how short in length that name may be for any entity who is progressing through the process of soul perfection in the earth plane of three-dimensional materiality. Obviously, this indicates that each entity in the present incarnation has at some time in a previous lifetime manifested and applied compassion toward another human being. Any of the nine numbers that is missing from the birth name translates into a karmic debt and lesson still to be learned in this lifetime.

Number One (1)

This number refers to the First Cause/Creative Forces or simply God because it pertains to beginnings of any kind. All activities emanate from the number 1. This is the number of the perfect sphere that has only one surface as a three-dimensional form and possesses the same diameter, omnidirectionally. Many people, as a consequence of our natural ego and free-will birthright, intensely desire to be "number 1", but they should be striving to add a cipher to the 1 because 10 is the number of Perfection, which is the destiny of the spiritual soul.

When applied to humankind and the personal Self, descriptive words are individualistic, independent, pioneering, ambitious, self-centered, innovative, inventive, original, self-confident, impulsive, willful, creative, initiative and leadership. (Note: Since human nature can be polarized and dualistic, these descriptive traits can be either positive or negative, or a combination of both in varying degrees.)

Number Two (2)

This number refers to dualism, which appears to be the basic nature of our local universe, albeit three (3) is the real or wholistic nature. While the number 2 makes for strength, it also pertains to weakness, such as a bipod versus a tripod, which also involves stability. Our whole world/globe is bipolar with its two hemispheres, much like a human physical brain. Consider the ideological differences between East and West, which appear to be increasing at this crucial time in the spiritual evolution of humankind, and the philosophy and prophecy of the Mayan Sacred Calendar/Tzolkin, as spiritually-interpreted by Dr. Carl Johan Calleman, is indicating a complete reversal of the activities of the left and right hemispheres of the brain in human beings now. This now is very evident regarding the extreme materialism in China, India, and virtually all of Asia that is shifting the balance of economic and military powers from the West, especially concerning the United States of America. Of course, the greatest duality of the number 2 is the struggle between our Free Will (birthright) and the Supreme Will of God or Creative Forces, as the Edgar Cayce spiritual source always referred to as the Source of everything! Jesus/Jeshua the Christ preferred the more personal term of "Father."

When applied to the personality of an individual, descriptive words are partnership, cooperation, companionship, association, friendliness, diplomacy, service, harmony, receptivity and adaptability.

Examples of the number 2 are:

1. Male and female genders.
2. The yin-yang feminine and masculine passive and active principles in nature.
3. The positive and negative polarity in magnetism and electricity.
4. The positive and negative halves of a sine wave for alternating current.
5. Intellect and intuition.
6. The immutable, universal law of cause-and-effect

Number Three (3)

This is the number of wholeness, such as the primary Holy Trinity that is comprised of Father, Son and Holy Spirit. The Master Soul, as the Christ, placed great emphasis on the number 3 while teaching the Christ Philosophy to His specially-chosen twelve disciples. It is the number of the triangle, which is the first plain figure required to construct the first of the geometric solids (the sphere is already perfect), which is the tetrahedron, the building block of matter and the most important of the five Pythagorean geometric solids. Indeed, Pythagoras employed the triangle to construct his very special and symbolic tetractys. The Edgar Cayce spiritual source was quite succinct with its triangular philosophy of life: "The spirit is the life; mind is the builder, and the physical is the result." This certainly is a concise diagnosis for any human physical or mental illness. Since each human being or entity is comprised of spirit/soul, mind and body that relate to our mental, emotional and physical nature, then we should think of ourselves as a Triangle of Being. This condition can be extrapolated to include a natal numeroscope and natal horoscope which, when portrayed as two intersecting triangles, create a Star of David pattern that illustrates the cosmic principle of "as above, so below." The numerological triangle denotes the three primary factors or aspects that are derived from the person's birth date, birth name and functional name. The astrological triangle depicts the three primary factors called the Sun Sign, Rising Sign/Ascendant and the Moon Sign. All six factors produce and yield an ideal source of knowledge and information that reveal an entity's true identity, as well as a "road map" that can guide the person successfully throughout the vicissitudes of life in Schoolhouse Earth. These spiritual sciences can indicate the proper and best action to initiate, as well as the corresponding best time factor for accomplishing the task and mission.

When applied to the personality of a person, descriptive words are expression, communication, sociability, teaching, writing, artistic talent, loquacity, inspiration and friendliness.

Examples of the importance of the number 3 and the triad are:

1. To perhaps necessarily reiterate, the triangular nature of human beings is comprised of spirit, mind and body, expressed as mental, emotional and physical aspects.

4

2. The human brain/mind is also three-phase, being divided into the conscious, subconscious and super-conscious, or *soul* mind, where memories of past-life experiences are stored and which can be accessed via dreams, meditation, prayer and other altered states of consciousness.

3. The three dimensions and three states of matter of the material plane of Earth, and it is spatially located as the third planet from our sun, which, because of its bright-light intensity, probably was phonetically named "Sun" as a form of archetype that depicts the Light-of-the-World, the *Son* of God.

4. Space, time and matter.

5. Astrologically, the first three "personal planets" of Mercury, Venus and Mars correspond to the mental, emotional and physical aspects of human beings, respectively.

6. Regarding meditation, the "third eye" or pineal endocrine gland is responsive during a required or sufficient degree of spiritual focus.

7. The three present primary Piscean Age religions of Judaism, Christianity and Islam that constantly compete with one another regarding their philosophy, validity and understanding of their true Source.

8. The proper balance of the three essential fatty acids, omega-3, omega-6 and omega-9, that the human body needs.

The nine basic numbers are divided into three triads (1-4-7, 2-5-8, 3-6-9), and the Edgar Cayce spiritual source indicated that the 3-6-9 triad is the most potent in the affairs of humankind, and this appears to be correct and appropriate regarding the spiritual evolution and destiny of all of humankind.

Number Four (4)

This number pertains to work, foundation, organization, the square and the base of a pyramid, and it also refers to the four basic elements of earth, air, water and fire that astrology also utilizes for a broader interpretation and understanding of the natal horoscope.

When applied to the human personality and its mundane affairs, descriptive words are work, order, foundation, organization, construction, form, practicality, stability, effort, endurance, pragmatism, duty, patience, discipline and exactitude.

Examples of the number 4 are:

1. The four elements of earth, air, water and fire.
2. The four geographic directions and locations.
3. The four gospels of the Holy Bible.
4. The four horsemen of the apocalypse in the final Book of Revelation.
5. The four equilateral triangles that comprise the tetrahedron, which is the first Pythagorean geometric solid that appears to be the most important configuration regarding three-dimensional nature. Indeed, a "channeled" spiritual source revealed that levitation/antigravity could be created from the effect that is produced when four (4) noble gas beams of energy are directed at the four vertices of a tetrahedron, and the mixture of the gases is important. (Incidentally, perhaps this is the methodology that the Atlanteans employed because the Edgar Cayce spiritual source revealed that this originating red race used levitation in their propulsion systems for all ground and water modes of transportation, and Reading 364-4 in 1932 referred to their use of special gases.)

Number Five (5)

This number is associated with many aspects of life because it denotes the five senses, and is even designated as the *number* of man. It also applies to the expanded four basic elements where the subatomic ether is added to earth, air, water and fire. Surprisingly, a "channeled" spiritual source stated that all atomic matter is the result of compacted ether! Moreover, the pyramid shape, which has five sides, apparently is a very efficient focusing configuration for the ether, as Kirlian electrical photography convincingly portrays (see Chapter 5). The prefix *pyr* pertains to fire and the *amid* means in the middle, which pretty much says it all. Numerologically, the number 5, as stated, pertains to humankind, whereas the number 9 is the *symbol* of man, according to the metaphysically-oriented Pythagoreans of ancient Greece.

When applied to the human personality, descriptive words are freedom, independence, variety, sensuality, change, versatility, adaptability, flexibility, diversity, activity, speculation, creativity, worldliness and adventurousness.

Examples of the omnipresence and pervasiveness of the number 5 in human life are:

1. The five races, senses, fingers, toes and facial openings.
2. The five basic geometric solids, as illustrated by Pythagoras.
3. The normal human body temperature is 98.6 (= 23/5) degrees Fahrenheit, and the ideal human ambient temperature is 68 (= 14/5) degrees Fahrenheit.
4. Human beings have 32 (= 5) teeth, 16 above and 16 below.

5. The human body has 32 (= 5) basic chemical building blocks.
6. Water freezes at 32 (= 5) degrees Fahrenheit and boils at 212 (= 5) degrees Fahrenheit.
7. Human bodies have 23 (= 5) pairs of chromosomes.
8. An Earth solar year is comprised of 365 (= 14/5) full days.
9. The five noble gases in Group 18 (9) of the Periodic Table of the Elements (the sixth gas in this grouping is radon, but it merely masquerades as a noble gas—do not breathe it because it is very carcinogenic). Note: Humankind is just beginning to appreciate the full benefit and versatility of the noble gases, especially *xenon*, which is the noblest of them all. Few people are aware that every breath of air that they inhale contains about .09 (human destiny number) parts of xenon in one million parts of air. Esoteric information indicates that even human consciousness could be raised if Earth's atmosphere contained a little more of xenon.
10. Metaphysical knowledge refers to the five bodies of energy pertaining to the paraphysical and parapsychological energies.
11. Esoteric knowledge describes the fifth (5) dimension as "bioplasma" (regarding light?) in a different time zone of this life spectrum (humankind).

Number Six (6)

This number refers primarily to the six days of Creation mentioned in the first book (Genesis) of the Holy Bible in which the First Cause/Creative Forces/God materialized planet Earth, but this time factor may be construed regarding a solar day of twenty-four hours. It also pertains to the sixth hour (12 noon) during the Crucifixion scenario concerning the great responsibility that Jesus/Jeshua the Christ assumed regarding

His demonstration of the ultimate act of becoming Love individualized. The number 6 also refers to the hexagonal Star of David on the national flag of Israel, which may be interpreted as two vertical intersecting triangles that represent "as above, so below." A tested spiritual source informed a sincere, dedicated group of spiritual seekers that six (6) is the *number* of Israel because this is the number of responsibility and adjustments. Perhaps this is the reason that the number 6 was included, and even triplicated (666), in the final book (Revelation) of the Holy Bible.

When applied to the human personality and activities, descriptive words are service, domesticity, emotionalism, guardianship, security, counseling, and, to reiterate, responsibility and adjustments.

Examples of the number six (6) in life and human interactions are:

1. The hexagonal symmetry pervasive in nature.
2. The six-sided hexagram.
3. The omega-6 fatty acid found in many foods that people excessively consume to the point of inducing an imbalance between the omega-3, omega-6 and omega-9 fatty acids that human physiology requires.
4. Concerning spiritual philosophy, a metaphysical source cited the six (6) "physical force fields of material creation", and also that the sixth (6) dimension is "bioplasmatic intelligence from a superspectrum coming back into our localized spectrum of evolving biological and anatomical form." This manifestation is extremely difficult for unenlightened humans to comprehend from our very limited three-dimensional reality, but perhaps a member of the Academy for Future Science (Ava, Missouri) could offer a satisfying elucidation for any inquisitive person.

Number Seven (7)

Being the dual number of mind and spirit, it can be easily understood why this number is mentioned (quoting a Bible scholar) fifty-two times in the very mysterious, phantasmagorical, complex and symbolical last book (Revelation) of the Holy Bible. Alternatively, we learn in the very first book (Genesis) of the same Bible that God "rested" on the seventh (7) day following Creation. Hence, this number has a strong affinity with the daily resting period (at least seven hours) that the human anatomy requires for regeneration and restoration of optimal energy, and this number especially applies to the seven (7) endocrine glands that correspond to the seven (7) main charkas or spiritual energy centers of the human body/temple. Moreover, the number seven (7) appears numerous times in the Book of Genesis (beginning), so it becomes obvious that the Creator is definitely indicating that any reader should pay attention to this very spiritual number. Indeed, the resurrected Christ appeared for the third and last time to only seven (7) of the twelve disciples (John 21) just before His ascension.

When the number seven is applied to the human personality and activities, descriptive words are spirituality, study, intellect, introspection, meditation, rest, intuition, wisdom, aloneness, peace, balance, silence, faith, analysis and research.

Examples of the number seven (7) are:

1. The seven colors of the light spectrum, as revealed via a prism.
2. The seven basic notes of the musical scale.
3. Complete renewal of all cells in the human body every seven years, which is the *physical* cycle, according to the Cayce spiritual source.
4. The seven years required to fully develop the human

brain, the fourteen (2 x 7) years required to fully develop the reproductive system and the twenty-one (3 x 7) years to fully develop the human musculoskeletal system and structure to finally attain human adulthood.

5. Religious ritualistic orders involve the number seven and the 7-unit candelabra.

6. The seven special foods that God gave to Moses and the Israelites concerning the promised lands (Deuteronomy 8:8, and 8 is the material number). Note: Continuing nutritional research and the Edgar Cayce spiritual source have confirmed the important, exceptional nutritional values of these seven (7) foods, with the pomegranate being the latest evaluation and validation. Regarding the "vines" (grapes) of the seven special foods, the Cayce source stated that the human body can be fully detoxified via a three-day (the whole number, of course) ingestion or "fast" of only Concord grapes. However, since Concord grapes are so perishable and unavailable out of season, perhaps any purple or dark red type of grape may be substituted, along with the easily accessible Concord grape juice. (Incidentally, the Cayce spiritual source also recommended consumption of only raw apples, specifically the Jonathan or sheep-nose variety, such as the Red Delicious, for a three-day period, then followed by ingestion of some olive oil as a final cleansing process for the fast.)

Number Eight (8)

The number eight pertains to all aspects of materiality, such as money, business, property and possessions. It also pertains to power at all levels, including authority, leadership and world governments, just as does the zodiacal sign of Capricorn, and this is being mentioned because the recent entry of both Jupiter (all of 2008) and Pluto (to 2024) into Capricorn should have a powerful effect on global businesses and world governments and their leaders and rulers. Jupiter pertains to expansiveness, sometimes to excess (think *derivatives*), and Pluto involves consciousness and transformation. Couple this scenario with the present finishing phase (ends in early February, 2011) of the very materialistic 8th Creation (Galactic) Cycle of the Mayan Sacred Calendar/Tzolkin and we obtain an appalling recipe for disaster, such as Christ described in Matthew 24 of the Holy Bible. Moreover, other astrological planetary aspects will be compounding the whole prospective scenario.

When applied to human personalities and activities, descriptive words are wealth, banking, construction, ambition, secularism, material success, administration and business of any nature.

Examples of the number eight (8) are:

1. The octagon and octagonal road signs.
2. The normal eight hours of work, recreation and rest/sleep for humans.
3. The diameter of Earth is approximately 8,000 miles, not being a perfect sphere.
4. The big business and economic World Group of Eight (G-8) that is comprised of members from the eight most financially-powerful nations and who try to manage/control global financial affairs.
5. According to the Cayce spiritual source, there are eight (!) dimensions to our solar system (versus the *nine* dimensions of our local universe, according to the spiritual information that was imparted to Dr. James J. Hurtak and later transcribed in The Book of Knowledge: The Keys of Enoch (consult the Academy for Future Science in Ava, Missouri).

Number Nine (9)

The number nine (9) emphatically pertains to human beings and their mandatory terrestrial process of soul development that is intended to culminate in a spiritualized state of Perfection by becoming Love individualized, just as Jesus/Jeshua the Christ demonstrated and manifested via His crucifixion ordeal that was predestined. This is the number of the humanitarian, and possibly even martyrdom, depending on the karmic status and mission of an entity. Any person whose total numbers/numerals of the official, accurate date of birth add to a number that reduces to the number 9 has entered embodiment in this incarnation with the assignment and intention of attempting to complete his/her earthly sojourns by denying the ego and sacrificing the self for their fellow human beings. There are numerous spiritual sources now that are revealing that humankind is nearing the end of its predestined spiritual evolution, so there are many people with the number 9 as a spiritual lesson and mission who are present in the earth plane at this crucial time, but the increasing, exacerbating, negative, global material conditions are seriously obstructing the pathway to a successful completion of their mission.

The qualifying factors regarding the completion of the Master Plan of the Holy Trinity were enumerated by Christ in Matthew 24 and the Book of Revelation of the Holy Bible, but the celestial and cosmic phase has yet to materialize, at least to a cognizant degree regarding humankind's awareness, albeit the spiritual teachers cited and quoted in this book have described the vast changes in cosmic conditions that presently are manifesting in at least our local universe. Hopefully, this will not necessitate the dire scenario wherein a large asteroid or comet veers to a collision course with our mother Earth.

Nine (9) is the *cycle* of man and the cyclic number, and it pertains to endings of any kind. Whereas the number 9 is the *destiny* number for humankind via the *process* of perfection, the number 10 pertains to perfection itself, which is the destiny of the Soul, as the great metaphysician, Pythagoras, illustrated with his triangular tetractys (the "tet" syllable refers to its four rows of numbers.)

Empirical information is indicating an increasing pervasiveness of the number 9 and its two multiples, 18 and 27 (triplication of the number 9) in the affairs of humankind, if only they would notice and engender a number 9 consciousness, as spiritual forces are fervently hoping will manifest broadly. The relatively-new, global, brain-taxing numbers game called "Sudoku" is based on the number 9, and many time-factored projects have deadlines that are set for the 27th of a month, indicating a big ending.

When the number nine (9) is applied to human activities and the personality, descriptive words are humanitarianism, altruism, brotherhood, universality, charity, compassion, selflessness, philanthropy, empathy, generosity, tolerance and understanding.

Examples of the number nine (9) are:

1. The normal gestation period to create a human being is 9 months.
2. The normal heart/pulse rate is 72 (= 9) beats per minute.
3. There are 9 planets in our solar system, regardless of the recent demotion of Pluto to a so-called "dwarf planet" by spiritually-ignorant astronomers. If only they knew its *real* purpose concerning the spiritual evolution of humankind, as defined in this book.
4. The perfect circle has 360 (9) degrees, and the perfect sphere has 360 (9) degrees, omnidirectionally.
5. Each American's social security number has 9 digits.
6. The U.S.A. postal ZIP code was lengthened from 5

(number of man) digits to 9 digits, thereby producing the number 9 human destiny vibration.

7. The recommended daily consumption of fruits and vegetables for optimal health has been increased from 5 to 9 servings per day.

8. The U.S. Supreme Court has 9 justices, including the often pivotal chief justice.

9. The world's greatest prophet and philosopher, Jesus/Jeshua of Nazareth, was crucified at the ninth (9) hour.

10. There are 72 (9) names of God or Infinite Mind.

11. Press number 9 on a telephone pad to end a call.

12. Typical human colloquialisms are "Cloud 9", "Love Potion #9", "the whole 9 yards", "Rule #9", "9 lives of a cat", "a stitch-in-time saves 9", "dressed-to-the-9s" and even a "9-day wonder."

13. The 9 major physiological systems in the human body.

14. About 99% of Earth's crust is composed of 9 elements.

15. The extremely important pineal endocrine gland (the so-called "third eye" that produces the sleep-regulating hormone, melatonin) is connected to the 9th thoracic of the spinal column.

16. The human body needs 20 amino acids, but produces only 11 naturally, thus requiring the other 9 to be externally obtained via nutrition.

17. The complete human chakra system, both internal (7) and external (2) has 9 energy centers.

18. The 9 muses of the liberal arts and sciences in Greek mythology.

19. The ancient Enneagram (9) regarding sacred psychology pertained to 9 human limiting character fixations.

20. The Catholic novena (9) requires a total of 9 days of prayer.

21. The Pentecost experience for the 12 (Judas had been replaced) disciples of Christ began at 9 o'clock in the morning and their daily prayer time began at the 9th hour (3 p.m.).

22. The increasingly popular human sport of baseball, which focuses on the individual, involves 9 players on each team, 9 innings, 90 feet between the bases, and even a ball circumference of 9 inches. The 3 strikes and 3 outs may unconsciously represent the whole number 3 of the Holy Trinity, and the so-called "seventh (7 is the number of mind and spirit and also rest) inning stretch" may represent the seventh (7) day that God rested in the Genesis account of the initial Creation of Earth.

23. Record-breaking athletes had the number 9 imprinted on their uniforms, viz., Ted Williams (last .400 baseball hitter); Roger Maris (first baseball player to hit 61 homeruns *in a single season*); Mia Hamm (scored more soccer goals for the U.S.A. than any other woman), and Wayne Gretsky, called "The Great One" (had *double* 9 on his uniform). Even movie actor, Robert Redford, chose number 9 for his uniform (per script?) in the baseball film, 'The Natural', in which he portrayed a magnificent homerun-king and slugger.

24. The word *love* vibrates to the number 9, as well as the *time* number (3+6+4+5 = 18 = 9).

25. Medical research has revealed that the blood analysis for anyone who has ingested pig/hog/ swine meat in any form will show that the blood characteristics will be similar to that of a cancer patient for up to nine (9) hours. No wonder that the Israelites were forbidden by God to eat pig meat. Hence, it becomes obvious why Jesus/Jeshua sent the exorcised demons into a herd of pigs that immediately drowned themselves. This may have seemed like a great waste to the Gentile owners, but we may surmise that all or most

of the pigs were infected or diseased. Indeed, reported statistics reveal that Jews have a lower incidence of cancer, but perhaps not in America because it is a Cancer Sun Sign nation, which may be a factor for why the frightening physical affliction of cancer is so prevalent in the U.S.A.

This completes the discussion regarding the nine basic numbers in the system of the spiritual science of numerology. However, there are four so-called *master* numbers, viz., 11, 22, 33 and 44, which are merely a duplication of the numbers 1, 2, 3 and 4. Until recently, only the number 11, which pertains to illumination and enlightenment, and the number 22, which pertains to the master builder, were available in numerology. The master number 33, which pertains to the 33rd degree in Freemasonry and is called the Christ number, and the master number 44, which pertains to mastery of mind and body, have been added as a normal evolutionary progression of this spiritual science. Correspondingly, the other primary spiritual science of astrology recently has added specific *asteroids* to its repertoire, but this appears to be superfluous because the basic planets and their aspects, and with the Sun and Moon (capitalized for astrology), are completely sufficient to describe, delineate and elucidate all of humankind's behavior and idiosyncrasies. So we must not get "lost in the stars."

Perhaps the reader has observed that the nine (9) basic numbers and the four (4) master numbers total to thirteen (13) numbers, which correspond with the transformational spiritual group that was comprised of Christ and the specially-chosen twelve (12) disciples, and 12 is the number of perfect structure, such as the basic measurements of the *new* Jerusalem mentioned in the Book of Revelation. This may be further extrapolated to include the significance, symbolism and purpose of the thirteen (13) original American colonies that began as a religious, spiritual

17

and sociological experiment that obviously was predestined to evolve into the quintessential democracy that obviously and definitely is still in its evolutionary process and condition, as has been illustrated so dramatically and painfully—virtually sado-masochistically—during the period 2000-2008.

CHAPTER TWO

The Meanings of Specific Multiple-Digit Numbers of the Spiritual Science of Numbers

Number Ten (10)

According to Manly P. Hall in his masterful, detailed, comprehensive metaphysical work, The Secret teachings of All Ages, the esoteric, philosophical teachings of the Pythagoreans centered on the number ten (10) as being both sacred and perfect. Hence, it may be assumed to be the *destiny* number of the spiritual Soul. It was viewed as the greatest of all numbers, so their special, symbolic Tetractys was a triangle with ten dots with tails (like human spermatozoa) positioned in four horizontal rows with one, two, three and four characters each, with the single dot near the top center and apex. The Edgar Cayce spiritual source applied the word "completeness" when referring to the meaning of the number 10, so this tends to validate this number as pertaining to the destiny of the soul, especially because it sequentially follows the human destiny number 9 that denotes merely the *process* of perfection of the soul.

Number Eleven (11)

In the first chapter it was stated that the number 11, as the first of the four master numbers, pertains to enlightenment and illumination. However, for many entities who have been assigned—and accepted—this higher numerical vibratory birth number and its associated life path/lesson, this energy level may be too high to comfortably assimilate and pursue. Thus, they may choose to function at the lower number 2 level, being a good friend, partner and listener, at least in the formative years of the life. It seems very likely that many 11s may have been motivated to fulfill their specific life mission during the long transit (1995 to January, 2008) of Pluto (consciousness and transformation) through the zodiacal sign of Sagittarius (solar 9th house of philosophy and higher education), which was accentuated by the accompanying presence of Jupiter (the "Great Benefic" of expansion) all during the initial year of the Pluto transit and even during the final year (2007) of this transforming planet in Sagittarius, which seems like a scenario involving a spiritual destiny conspiracy for all of humankind. Many 11s would have become teachers and writers of metaphysics during this recent long period, and there was a pervasive proliferation of New Age books, groups and organizations at that time, especially the unparalleled expansion of the Association for Research and Enlightenment of the Edgar Cayce Foundation. Moreover, since the solar 9th house strongly pertains to religions of any kind, perhaps some number 11s became religious leaders and facilitators, with some even establishing a type of New Age unorthodox church. Unfortunately, the greatly expansive influence of Jupiter can reach to a point of excess, so this explains the present religious fervor and friction in the world among the three (the whole number) primary Piscean Age religions of Judaism, Christianity and Islam, in order of appearance. Tragically, organized religions are often associated with ignorance, form and confusing symbolism that occasionally engender mistrust and even violence, as the appalling, total destruction of the twin World Trade Towers in New York City in 2001 so dramatically demonstrated and illustrated.

Number Twelve (12)

This number is emphasized in the Holy Bible, especially concerning the twelve tribes of Israel and the twelve disciples of Christ, and it is multiplied twelve times all the way up to 144,000 in the Book of Revelation where it refers to the total number of the 12,000 members of each of the twelve tribes of Israel. The number 12 is the mathematical basis for all perfect structure, as noted also in Revelation regarding the *new* city of Jerusalem. Even the numerical values of the three sides of the Pythagorean Divine Triangle (Life Theorem) add to twelve units (3, 4 and 5 = 12). Additionally, the fifth and last geometric solid of Pythagoras is the dodecahedron that is comprised of twelve pentagons. The solar year is divided into twelve months and each day into twelve hours for daytime and nighttime and twelve hours of daylight and darkness at the two equinoxes. There are twelve signs of the zodiac that are associated with twelve solar houses, and these pertain to twelve basic human personality types ranging from Aries to Pisces. There are twelve inches to a foot, and these inches apply to the measurements in the Great Pyramid in Egypt with a transposition factor of only one-thousandth (.001) of an English inch.

In Dr. James J. Hurtak's extremely provocative, mind-boggling, spiritual and scientific book, The Book of Knowledge: The Keys of Enoch, it mentions twelve meridians of Light that are connected to the "seed crystal", which is the "third eye" (pineal endocrine gland) in the head of a human being. It associates this with the "planetary computer" that has twelve Light focal channels regarding the "reprogramming" of human creation, which the Mayan Sacred Calendar/Tzolkin appears to indicate will occur during the crucial ending year of 2012 that should involve a scenario whereby the physical and chemical composition of three-dimensional human bodies will be transformed into fifth-dimensional (transcending the fourth dimension of *time)* "Whole Light Beings" that will establish the new "fifth root race" that even the Edgar Cayce spiritual source had mentioned way back in the 1930s. This tends to validate and even reinforce the designation of the number 5 as being the *number* of man.

21

Number Thirteen (13)

This is a strong spiritual number, beginning with Christ and the twelve disciples. Unfortunately, its potency long ago had induced such a high degree of fear that even the word, *triskaidekaphobia*, was created to accommodate and elucidate its fear. Apparently, the founding fathers of America had no fear of the number 13 because the country was formed from thirteen original colonies, which appears to have been predestined. Perhaps being at least subliminally or unconsciously aware of the full spiritual significance and important meaning of this number, it was indirectly displayed all over the Great Seal of the United States of America and even onto its currency or legal tender, and even to the thirteen red and white stripes of its national flag and identity bearer. In addition to the thirteen stars, thirteen arrows, thirteen olive tree leaves and thirteen stripes on the shield, the symbolic pyramid (fire-in-the-middle) has thirteen steps or courses of masonry. Even the words, *E PLURIBUS UNUM* (one out of many) and *ANNUIT COEPTIS* (He hath prospered our beginnings) contain thirteen letters each.

Number Seventeen (17)

An entire book could be written solely concerning the number 17 and its relevance to the spiritual evolution of humankind, starting with the human-eradicating Flood in Genesis, which is the very first book and story of the Holy Bible (see next chapter). The number 17 appears prominently in many chapters of this book that pertain to the primary spiritual theme of the Holy Bible , Great Pyramid, Mayan Sacred Calendar/ Tzolkin, Pythagorean Divine Triangle (Life Theorem), Fatima Prophecy, and especially to the birth, evolution and destiny of the United States of America. Since the biblical Flood began on the seventeenth (17) day of a month (Genesis 7:11), it seems obvious that this seemingly unusual number pertains to *suffering*. However, Noah's great ark grounded on a mountain in Ararat again on the seventeenth (17) day of the seventh month, so this obviously now also pertains to *redemption*. But since Noah and his family had to endure many months of suffering on that crowded ship with all those malodorous, noisy animals and birds, this denotes that humankind needs to experience a lengthy period of suffering before redemption will be offered from Creative Forces or God.

The number nine (9) evolutionary process of perfection represents this arduous period of transformation. The Edgar Cayce spiritual source described this process quite succinctly when it stated that each "sojourn" in the earth plane is an "experience" for the soul, and this obviously would necessitate the atonement for and dissipation of any negative karma/debts that had manifested in one or more previous incarnations in the material earth plane. Moreover, the number 17 appears to have been derived from the coupling of the number 8 of materiality and the humanitarian and human destiny number 9 which signifies that the soul only can be perfected by its mode of processing through the earth plane of matter. The Pythagorean Divine Triangle, when interpreted *wholistically*, illustrates this hypothesis very well, as does Dr. Carl Johan Calleman in his spiritual interpretation of the Mayan Sacred Calendar/Tzolkin. (Incidentally, it certainly is interesting that the name *God* vibrates to the number 17 because the letters, when converted to their associated numbers of 7-6-4, add to that numerical value, and many people view God as a strict and stern paternal Creator who makes them suffer, sometimes intolerably and unjustly.)

To justify and validate this author's interpretation and hypothesis concerning the suffering aspect of the number 17, the following personal episodes should tend to support and substantiate this:

In 1985, before I became aware of the spiritual meaning and purpose of the number 17, my wife and I rented a house with the number 17 affixed to it. I was quite pleased because, numerologically, this number reduces and vibrates to the material and money number 8, and at that time I was trying to accumulate the funds I would need to purchase a house to establish a permanent (?) home. Not long after we moved into this number 17 house, an extended rainy period swelled the heretofore almost dried up stream near this house to a high level that inundated the basement of the house. We took turns bailing water for a mandatory period of nine (9!) days and nights until the water receded and also before I would have to "build an ark."

The following year, I was standing at the kitchen sink one day when I heard thunder in the distance. I began to think about the Cayce spiritual information that stated, "The best description of God is *electricity*." (my italics) Suddenly, a bolt of lightning struck the large pine tree adjacent to the house. However, the only electrical circuit breaker that was tripped was connected to the kitchen where I was standing when "God spoke to me", it seemed.

Since three is the whole number of Holy Trinity, there obviously needed to be one more concluding experience for me in this number 17 domicile. About two years later, I "invested" in some silver bullion—silver and gold are the only genuine form of money in the Holy Bible—but the poor timing and my investing neophyte status at that time, especially regarding so-called "margin", resulted in my having to file for bankruptcy and my coerced removal from that horrible number 17 house.

Actually, my negative experiences with the number 17 began from my physical birth in this lifetime because for the first seventeen (17) years of my life I had been told by my parents that I had been born on March 4th and my given birth name was *Parker*, a name that I grew to detest because of all the negative, hurtful remarks that this name elicited from my schoolmates and associates. However, at age seventeen (17) I obtained a copy of my birth certificate that revealed both that I had been born on the *third* day of March and that my full birth name was William Parker Maynard. I released a great sigh of relief, and thought, "This is wonderful because now I can be called *Bill!*" In retrospect, I now can realize how truly ignorant I was about this common—*really* common—nickname because it vibrates to the dreaded (at least for me) number 17 (2+9+3+3), which is associated with suffering, generally, but there still is for me the hope of *redemption*.

To illustrate that the number 17 is still "following me around", on February 17, 2006, my 17-year-old granddaughter, whom I was legal guardian for, begged me to co-sign an auto loan for her. Being a Friday and the dreaded number 17, I implored her to wait until Monday, but she said she had to have the car for the weekend. Being a number 9/Pisces (the quintessential "sucker" sign that showman P.T. Barnum must have been referring to when he said, "There's one born every minute!"), I soon succumbed and signed the loan document. At any rate, only seven months later she somehow (a loose term when applied to a teenager) struck a tree and the Subaru—can you believe this?—burst into flames and was totally destroyed just after she had exited the vehicle. [Incidentally, the adolescent age of seventeen is arguably the most difficult year for many humans because at age 17 most children are in their last year of high school—at least in America—and are anguishing about their final grade and what institution of higher learning they can qualify to attend or what they will do when they leave high school. Moreover, this is a high-mortality, vehicular "accident" year, and no human under age 18 (the *time* number) truly has manifested enough responsibility to properly guide an automobile, and also to conform to the vehicular laws of society.]

A final commentary regarding my present and ongoing encounter with the number 17 concerns my current residence. When I bought this property in 1996, it had no house number, only a mail box number. Then, the emergency 911 system required that all residential houses would be assigned a facilitating ambulance location number, which engendered a bit of anxiety in me, and this proved to be justified when my house was assigned the number 1475 (= 17). This number is compounded by my present postal ZIP code of 05732 (= 17 again) and its suffix of 9798 (= 33), and the combined numbers equal 50. The number 17 pertains to suffering, the master number 33 (the Christ number) pertains to great responsibility and adjustments, and the number 50 is the Pythagorean sacred number and is the same number that was affixed to my house in California in 1976 when I began my metaphysical and spiritual journey toward Enlightenment. It should be added that the U.S.A. is comprised of its present and finalized 50 individual states and the so-called King's Chamber in the Great Pyramid (a Bible in stone) is vertically located at the fiftieth (50) course of masonry/blocks.

Number Eighteen (18)

Being a product of 2 x 9 (the cyclic number), this number is specifically called the *time* number, albeit the numbers 9, 18 and 27 all pertain to the time factor regarding any situation or condition. If something does not end after the basic 9 years, it can continue for another 9-year cycle to 18 years, when it should experience a stronger ending process. If a third 9-year cycle is involved, then it can result in even a traumatic ending process, such as the global events of the number 27/9 world year of 1989 (end of Berlin Wall and the disintegration of Soviet domination of Europe and actually the beginning of the end of the Soviet Union itself). The number 18 appears numerous times in the affairs of humankind, denoting significant endings that induce new beginnings.

Examples of the number 18 as a time factor are:

1. The American Revolutionary War began on April 18, 1775, when silversmith Paul Revere began his famous horse ride to warn the militia against the British (actually, William Dawes was reported to have completed the warning ride to Lexington after Revere had been detained by a British patrol).
2. The final battle at Waterloo to finally defeat Napoleon was on June 18, 1815, albeit the series of battles had begun on June 16 of that month.
3. The devastating San Francisco earthquake occurred on April 18, 1906.
4. Long dormant Mt. St. Helens in California surprisingly erupted on May 18, 1980, which involved both a number 18 day in a number 18 (1+9+8+0) world year for added emphasis.
5. The first "walk in space" occurred on March 18, 1965, by a Russian cosmonaut.
6. The great physicist, Albert Einstein, transitioned back to the spirit realm on April 18, 1955.
7. The very successful Broadway musical, "Cats", ended its long run after 18 years.
8. The Star Trek television series ended in 2005 after 18 years.
9. A large asteroid finally was detected at only 26,000 miles from Earth on March 18, 2004 (Sun in Pisces and its associated solar 12th house of self-undoing).

10. Jesus/Jeshua disappears at age 12 and reappears 18 years later to begin His predestined ministry that was intended to demonstrate how each human must become Love individualized.

11. Abraham Lincoln issued his Emancipation Proclamation on January 1, 1863, which was a number 18 (1+8+6+3) world year. He desperately wanted to make it official in 1862 (a number 17 world year of suffering) based on the Union Pyrrhic victory at Antietam Creek in Maryland, but the time number 18 obviously needed to be involved regarding sinful slavery.

12. The time number 18 world year of 1863 also pertained to the American Civil War Battle of Gettysburg (July) that altered the course of the war leading to the fall of the Confederacy.

13. The Russian Bolshevik Revolution began in 1917, a number 18 world year.

14. Oil was discovered in Persia (now Iran) in 1908, a number 18 world year.

15. The Texas battle for independence (actually confiscation) at the Alamo occurred on March 6 (the final assault) in 1836, which was not only a number 18 world year, but all the digits of the date (3-6-1-8-3-6) total to 27 (triplicated number 9), the number of strong and final endings. Moreover, Sun in Pisces assured the coup de grace via the solar 12th house of self-undoing, which is the same situation regarding the long, continuing idiotic Bush war in Iraq (Bush-whacked) that was initiated with a blitzkrieg ("shock-and-awe") during Sun in Pisces.

16. Long-dormant Mount Vesuvius erupted in 1944 (bomb vibrations?) which was a number 18 world year.

17. World War II D-day was on June 6, 1944, a number 18 world year and also on a number 6 day of responsibility and adjustments.

18. The Korean (mostly Chinese) War ended in 1953, a number 18 world year.

19. The first American astronaut in space occurred in 1962, a number 18 world year.

20. The year of 1908 (= 18) was called "the year that changed everything" because Henry Ford started the assembly line that mass-produced the Model T automobile and Wilbur Wright flew his airplane for an assumed world record of nearly two and one-half hours. The U.S. Navy sent its Great White Fleet around the globe to show the world that America had become a world power after its pretentious and highly-profitable war with Spain and now was ready to begin its imperialistic quest that was mandated via its "manifest destiny", at least as envisioned by "rough rider" President Theodore Roosevelt from his "bully pulpit."

Number Twenty-Seven (27)

Completing the triplication of the cyclic number 9 results in the number 27 of potent, big endings, and this number empirically appears to be used more frequently now, perhaps via a "spiritual conspiracy" to awaken humankind to its possible and probable physical transformation that may occur in the critical final year of 2012, as the collectively-interpreted Mayan Sacred Calendar/Tzolkin indicates. Indeed, when the true source of this spiritually-chronological calendar matrix is known to anyone (see Chapter 5), then it should be very seriously contemplated and studied.

Pertinent examples of the number 27 as a vibratory force to manifest endings are:

1. The massive volcano, Krakatoa, finally blew itself apart on August 27, 1883.

2. The three-year Korean (Chinese) War ended on July 27, 1953, which was a big ending in a time number 18 world year that also is prominent in the chronology of the Great Pyramid (see Chapter 4).

3. The military struggle in Vietnam ended in its eighteenth (time number 18) year, but a cease fire occurred on January 27, 1973, two years before the official ending. Moreover, the unfortunate country previously had been partitioned at the 17th (number of suffering) parallel.

4. Abraham Lincoln ordered all Union forces to attack the Confederacy on January 27, 1862.

5. Abraham Lincoln's assassin, John Wilkes Booth, was hunted down and killed on his twenty-seventh (27) birthday.

6. England's long-time prime minister, Tony Blair, voluntarily left office on June 27, 2007, which also was a number 9 world year of endings.

7. The fearsome, massive battleship, Bismarck, finally was sunk on May 27, 1941.

8. South African activist, Nelson Mandela, reportedly spent 27 years in prison until his release.

9. The New York City World Trade Towers were destroyed by Islamic terrorists in their twenty-seventh (27) year of existence.

10. As mentioned previously in the discussion for the number 18, the hated Berlin Wall finally was dismantled gleefully in 1989, a number 27 world year of big endings.

11. Pope Paul II died in his twenty-seventh (27) year of reign, long after surviving an assassination attempt in 1980, which was a time number 18 world year.

12. The gigantic aerial explosion at Tunguska, Siberia, on June 30, 1908, involved both the powerful-ending number 27 and the time number 18, i.e., addition of all the numerals in the date (6+3+0+1+9+0+8) results in 27 and 1+9+0+8 equals 18. [Note: Since no scientist to date adequately has explained the actual cause of the obviously massive explosion and its extensive peripheral destruction, some open-minded investigators have postulated that an extremely unusual electrical experiment by the recognized genius, Nikola Tesla, at his Long Island, New York, 187-foot-high "wireless electrical transmitter" had caused the Tunguska disaster, especially since Tesla had told the New York Times newspaper editor in both 1907 (= 17) and 1908 (= 18) that he could project destructive electrical energy to any point of the globe. Perhaps most likely having chosen a remote, isolated location near the North Pole for his test, the powerful beam of energy may have overshot the Pole and reached Tunguska, which is in a direct line to the test tower. In association with the characteristics of electricity, the skies over Europe manifested an eerie all-night glow for a few nights following the Siberian blast. Various theories have been postulated, including asteroids and comets, but the most interesting—and perhaps even plausible in this case— hypothesis involves the manifestation (inducement?) of a huge form of ball lightning that exploded.]

13. The American Boston Red Sox baseball team won their first "World Series" title in 86 years on October 27, 2004, which was 18 (time number) years since their previous World Series defeat on October 27, 1986. Ironically, the very last out of their 2004, 86-year victory, came from an opposing batter who had the number 3 on his uniform. This was the same number

that their renowned and adored homerun king, George Herman (Babe) Ruth, had worn on his uniform, and it had been believed, however superstitiously, for many decades that Ruth's spirit had manifested the so-called "Curse of the Bambino" because the owner of the Red Sox baseball team in 1918 had sold Babe Ruth to their despised rival, the New York Yankees, in order to obtain the money he needed to finance a personal theatrical endeavor that grossly deviated from America's beloved sport of baseball.

To add further credibility concerning the number 27 vibrational energy (as the Edgar Cayce spiritual source referred to the effect of numbers), a list of this author's personal experiences with the number 27 is submitted for the reader's consideration and contemplation.

1. My birth date of March 3, 1929, reveals an assigned—and reluctantly accepted?—life path/lesson of the number 27 when all six numerals are added, and this number is harmonious with my basic Pisces personality and character, especially when the 27 is reduced to the basic number 9 of humanitarianism, altruism and sacrifice, as I have come to woefully understand during long, arduous years, and my Scorpio Rising Sign/Ascendant (outer personality) assures that I will always persevere in my attempt to accomplish my purpose and specific mission in this incarnation/lifetime.

2. My Social Security Number, which discretion and trepidation preclude divulging, totals to 27.

3. My Military Service Number was RA11185380, which adds to the number 27.

4. My account number for a stock market "investment" was 80142273 (=27).

5. My account number for an automobile purchase loan was 2020014639 (=27).

6. A home mortgage loan had scheduled monthly payments of $239.67 (=27).

7. Another later home mortgage loan had scheduled monthly payments of $354.96 (=27).

8. I was married (almost 55 years ago) on November 27, 1953 (even a time number 18 year).

9. The vowels of my birth name, William Parker Maynard, when converted to numbers, are 9-9-1-1-5-1-1, which total to the number 27. In the system of numerology, the vowels of the birth name designate the *soul urge/motivation*, which is the second most important aspect of an entity's natal numeroscope. In this case, it amplifies and reinforces my 27/9 life purpose.

10. The order number (81301824) and confirmation number (120352815) for a recent integrated telephone-TV-Internet package each total and vibrate to the collective number 27.

11. On January 3, 1976 (1+3+1+9+7+6 = 27), I obviously was guided by Spirit to read the book Edgar Cayce: The Sleeping Prophet, that initiated my spiritual quest for the "holy grail."

12. I had not been in a hospital for an ailment my entire life nor had I been to a doctor in 27 years when I stressed my back to a degree of total immobility that resulted in my transport by ambulance to a local hospital in 2001 (my number 9 personal year of endings). Their treatment of morphine, ionizing X-radiation and "pain pills" was both antiquated and ignorant.

Thirty-Three (33)

In the evolutionary process of the important spiritual science of numerology, the number 33, as stated previously, recently has been added as the third master number (besides 11 and 22). This number is a very high vibration of the basic number 6 that pertains to responsibility and adjustments. It is called the "Christ number" in association with the accepted thirty-three (33) years that the Christ Soul, as Jesus/Jeshua of Nazareth, resided in physical embodiment in the earth plane. His previous and second incarnation, according to the Edgar Cayce psychic perusal of the Akashic Record or Book of Life, was as *Adam* (He called Himself the "Son of man" to validate this Cayce revelation) who had initiated our Adamic race of human beings that Dr. James J. Hurtak fully explains in his spiritually-dictated, astounding book, The Book of Knowledge: The Keys of Enoch. To further validate the concept and reality of reincarnation, Christ told the Jewish leaders during a heated altercation that He had been Melchizadek, the High Priest of God and King of Salem (city of peace) when He had been involved with Abram/Abraham (John 8:56, Genesis 14 and Hebrews 7).

Examples of the number 33 are:

1. The 33 degrees of Freemasonry.
2. The 33 vertebrae in the human spinal column at birth (the sacrum bones fuse together before the physical adulthood age of twenty-one, or three times the physical number 7).
3. The number 33 is an important chronological number in the Great Pyramid at Giza, Egypt, as cited in Chapter 4.
4. The Great Depression in the U.S.A. began with the stock market crash on "Black Tuesday" October 29, 1929 (1+0+2+9+1+9+2+9 = 33), which was an

emotionally-devastating day that initiated many years of painful responsibilities and adjustments that were manifested via the basic lower number 6 vibration. Moreover, the astrological factor of Sun in Scorpio (death and rebirth) obviously must have exacerbated the severity of this financial calamity, and this tends to validate the reason that global stock markets generally are in a precarious annual situation during late October.

5. According to Dr. J.J. Hurtak`s divinely-revealed information in the aforementioned book, humankind's spiritual evolution is in its final phase and will involve a metamorphic condition in which the 32 basic chemical building blocks of the human body will be coupled with a thirty-third (33) element, or implanting of "Divine Wisdom." This will alter the vibrations of the physical body and prepare it for "reincorporation" back into the "Divine Body." The Fatima Prophecy also revealed that humankind will undergo a physical transformation near the end of our pivotal evolution (see Chapter 7).

Number Forty (40)

This is the *testing* number all throughout the Holy Bible, beginning in Genesis (40 days of rain to create the human-annihilating Flood) and continuing to Satan's 40 days of his temptation of Jesus/ Jeshua, and even to the 40-day period during which the now resurrected Christ appeared to the disciples. The number 40 will be fully depicted in the next chapter regarding the Holy Bible.

Number Fifty (50)

The number 50 has a special meaning for humankind, as denoted in the Great Pyramid in Egypt, and the 50 stars in the American flag, its national symbol. The 50 collective, self-governing states of the United States of America represent the culmination of its geographical evolutionary process ("manifest destiny"). The Pythagorean Divine Triangle (Life Theorem), when its three sides of designated values of 3, 4 and 5 are squared, results in a total of 50 units or components, thus deriving the so-called Pythagorean Sacred Number of 50. The so-called King's Chamber in the Great Pyramid is vertically located at the fiftieth (50) course of masonry or blocks. One Bible researcher calls 50 the number of Jubilee and deliverance, which may be an accurate assessment of this special number.

This author's personal experiences with the number 50 are as follows:

1. I was residing in a number 50 house near San Diego, California, in early 1976 when I unexpectedly experienced a traumatic mystical encounter with the Christ Spirit, as described fully in the Introduction to this book. The date was January 3, 1976 (1+3+1+9+7+6 = 27/9!).
2. As of this writing, I still reside near Rutland, Vermont, at postal ZIP Code 05732-9798, and these nine (9) numbers add to 50, so to me this seems to validate the spiritual source that said that the numbers "have a tendency to follow you around." This remark appears to be quite appropriate concerning my numerous encounters with the number 17 that I merely touched upon in this chapter.

CHAPTER 3

The Language of the Numbers in the Holy Bible

In the very first chapter, Genesis, of the Old Testament of the Holy Bible, God/FirstCause/Creative Forces emphasized the number 7 (God/spirit) concerning the creation of heaven and earth, and the last emphasis of the number 7 is found in the Book of Revelation, the last book of the Bible in which the number 7 is cited 52 (=7) times, obviously to assure that humankind will "get the message." The most prominent reference to the number 7 in Revelation pertains to the seven (7) churches that the apostle Paul had established for the Gentiles, and the Edgar Cayce spiritual source revealed that the seven seals and seven churches symbolically represent the seven (7) human endocrine glands that are associated with the seven (7) human chakras or physical energy/vortex centers.

In Genesis 7, when Noah was six hundred years old, on the seventeenth (17 is the number of *suffering* here) day of the second month the rain began, and Noah entered the great ark with his family and seven (7) pairs of various animals and birds. It rained for forty (40) days and nights, which denotes the *testing* number. Again, on the seventeenth (17) day of the seventh (7) month the ark grounded on a mountain in Ararat, so here the number 17 obviously refers to *redemption* being offered after a long period of suffering in the earth plane of materiality, which certainly indicates that all of humankind must at some time experience the number 17 vibratory cleansing process. In the latter years of a lengthy human life, most entities will come to realize that *we learn best through suffering.* Noah then waited forty (testing number 40) days before releasing a raven to ascertain the presence of dry land below them, but it did not return. He then waited seven (7) days more and released a dove that did return. After another seven (7) days, he released the dove again and it returned with an olive leaf in its beak. After waiting even another seven (7) days, Noah released the dove again, but it never returned. Opening the hatch of the ship and seeing that the ground was dry, Noah and his family were ready to depart from the obvious misery of their long confinement, but God made them wait another two months (=9) until the entire earth was dry before they were permitted to leave the ark on the twenty-seventh (27) day of a month. Since the number 27 is the triplication of the cyclic number 9 of endings and also the human destiny number, it appears quite appropriate for this scenario of a very big ending (27) for this family of four males and four females (4 is the foundation number and 8 is the basic number of the material earth plane that human beings must experience).

Number Three (3)

The most important reference to the wholeness of the number 3 is certainly the triangular nature of the Holy Trinity that is comprised of Father, Son and Holy Spirit. The Son, Jesus/ Jeshua, repeatedly emphasized the number 3, much to the chagrin of at least the disciple, Peter the "Rock", who was chastised more than once by the Master. It appears evident that eventually all twelve (12 is the number of perfect structure and order) of the disciples came to understand the triangular full nature of Spirit, especially after they had absorbed and assimilated the full energy and power of the Holy Spirit at Pentecost after Christ had returned to the realm/dimension of spirit forty (40) days following His execution at Calvary/Golgotha.

The following information is a listing of the many references to the number 3 in the Holy Bible

Matthew 2:1 —The three (3) "wise men" (correctly called *astrologers* in The New English Bible, 1972 edition) appeared at the birth of the Master Soul/Christ into physical embodiment, and they presented three (3) gifts of gold, frankincense and myrrh.

Matthew 12:40—Jesus/Jeshua talks about Jonah, who had spent three (3) days and nights in the "belly" of a whale.

Matthew 17:1-2—Jesus/Jeshua takes the three (3) primary disciples, Peter, James and John (these three represented the body, mind and heart/emotions of Christ, respectively), up a mountain to witness His Transfiguration, and Moses and Elijah appear with Him (3 disciples and 3 prophets). On the way down the mountain, Jesus/Jeshua cites the reality of *reincarnation* by telling the disciples that Elijah had returned to physical embodiment as John the Baptist, who then had been beheaded by King Herod. Note: It would seem that the reason that John the Baptist was beheaded pertained to the time when he was in prison and sent one of his followers to ask Jesus/Jeshua if He really was the long-awaited Messiah, and this doubt may have been engendered by their familial relationship because John was the son of Mary's cousin, Elizabeth. Moreover, even the natural-born brothers of Jesus/Jeshua were very dubious of his divinity, but certainly not after the Crucifixion experience(s). The symbolism of the act of beheading shows that John's doubting and faithless brain/mind had to be separated from his physical body that represents the Temple of God/Spirit.

Again referring to the concept and reality of reincarnation, in Matthew 24 of The New English Bible the whole frightening scenario regarding the prophecy for the ending of the (Piscean) Age is terminated by Jesus/Jeshua predicting and explaining that "the present generation will live to see it all." Since the entire prophecy and scenario needs only for the celestial/cosmic conditions to occur for fulfillment, it would seem that Christ was saying that all people who were alive at that time would return to the earth plane again at this *present* time. This certainly applies to this author, as the Introduction to this book indicates. A valid question could be asked concerning reincarnation and its implausibility associated with the more than six billion people/souls now in the earth plane, but the Cayce spiritual source spoke of certain entities who had been in "other systems" of the universe(s) who now needed the experience of a three-dimensional influence for the completion of their evolutionary process for soul Perfection. Also consider the large populations of the now-submerged continents of Atlantis and Lemuria/Mu.

Matthew 26:34—Jesus/Jeshua tells Peter that he will deny Him three (3) times during their last night together before His execution/crucifixion.

Matthew 17:23—Jesus/Jeshua tells the disciples that He will be executed, but that He would arise from physical death on the third (3) day following this predestined martyrdom that would illustrate His becoming Love Individualized and that also would serve as an example for all humans to follow.

Matthew 26:36—Jesus/Jeshua takes the three primary disciples, Peter, James and John, to a place called Gethsemane where He prays alone three (3) separate times, but appears to the sleeping disciples after each prayer and chastises them for not staying alert. Since this was the night before His martyrdom for humankind, this scenario appears to symbolize—Christ used so much symbolism—that humankind will be "asleep" when He returns to the earth plane for His final mission, which may be imminent based on the appalling materialism of humankind and the over six billion entities here.

Mark 15:25-27—Jesus/Jeshua was crucified at the third (3) hour, which was 9 a.m., according to The New English Bible, and 9 is the number of endings. There were three (3) crosses at

Calvary, and three (3) nails—not four—were driven through the hands and feet of Christ.

Matthew 27:46—During the Crucifixion, the sky darkened at midday, the sixth (6) hour (number of *responsibility* and *adjustments*) and stayed dark for three (3) hours until the ninth (9) hour, or until 3 p.m., according to The New English Bible. Of course, the ending of the Christine Ministry had to involve the number 9 of endings when the Spirit of the physical man, even Jesus/Jeshua the Christ, departed from the human body. The scenario involving the *resurrected* Christ was a very different matter, as the totally-demoralized eleven (Judas had hanged himself) disciples later would realize.

John 21:15–17—At their third (3) meeting following the Resurrection, Jesus/Jeshua asked Peter three (3) separate times if he loved Him, irritating Peter considerably, while Christ obviously was reminding Peter of his lack of faith, determination and commitment when he had denied Him three (3) times during the long night of His arrest and interrogation, and subsequent torture.

Acts 2:15—After Judas had been replaced by the selected Matthias, the renewed twelve disciples met at the third (3) hour, which was 9 a.m., to receive the full, metaphysical power of the Holy Spirit that Christ had told them would be needed so as to accomplish their unique individual assignments for humankind, and the powerful spiritual energies at Pentecost were virtually overwhelming during their full assimilation by the mind and body, providing even the power for physical decorporation and teleportation.

Acts 3:1—The daily hour of prayer for the disciples was at the ninth hour, or 3 p.m., which was the same time when Jesus/Jeshua had returned to the dimension of spirit at Calvary.

Luke 3:23—This verse states that Jesus/Jeshua was *about* thirty (10 x 3) years of age when He reappeared after eighteen years (see below comment concerning the 18 time number) to begin His predestined spiritual ministry. This imprecise age time factor obviously is intentional and is quite significant because it most likely refers to the spiritual science of astrology that very seriously involves the *first* Saturn Return (karma, duty and *destiny*) that occurs for anyone at the age of 29.5years, and is strongly in effect between ages 29 and 30 because of the lengthy transit and orbit of Saturn around the sun. Hence, at this time in His life, Jesus/Jeshua would have been acutely aware at the Soul level (superconscious mind) of His destiny and singular mission for humankind.

Luke 2:42—When Jesus/Jeshua was only twelve (number of perfect structure) years of age, He began questioning and even teaching the Jewish religious leaders at the Temple in Jerusalem. His parents, Mary and Joseph, had been gone for a day during their return trip to Nazareth when they realized that the precocious young boy was not with their group of travelers. Returning to Jerusalem, it took them three (3) days to locate the young Messiah. Then this same Chapter 2 concludes by merely stating that He grew in wisdom and stature, and Chapter 3 (number of *expression*) begins the ministry of Jesus/ Jeshua. So the logical, irritating, and perhaps necessary—unless you possess blind faith—question that this situation should engender is: What happened during those so-called "lost eighteen years" (18 is the *time* number)?

There are spiritual sources that offer a seemingly satisfactory elucidation to this mystery, and the Christ Philosophy advises that if we seek we will find the answers to life's riddles and mysteries. The Aquarian Gospel of Jesus the Christ provides a believable and satisfying account of the full thirty-three (33) years of the life of Jesus/Jeshua of Nazareth and His divine ministry for the plight of humankind, but the Edgar Cayce spiritual source gives us a thoroughly-detailed, comprehensive account that was obtained from the Akashic Record (Book of Life) that contains the events of every lifetime/incarnation for every human being. The numerous, detailed psychic readings for all of the (30?) earthly appearances—not all in normal physical form—of the Christ Soul are very credible and convincing to thousands of highly-educated, professional, discerning individuals, which obviously is the reason why the Association for Research and Enlightenment of the Edgar Cayce Foundation attracts so many international theologians (all religions), philosophers, scientists and doctors with Ph. D.s, M.D.s, etc. Empirical and anecdotal information reveals how so many lives, especially incarcerated entities, have been transformed via the consciousness-raising effects of the thousands of astounding Cayce psychic readings, perhaps because the common denominator and central theme of the great majority of these spiritual readings is Jesus/Jeshua the Christ and the Holy Trinity in general. Indeed, the Cayce spiritual information was the initial catalyst for the composing of this book.

Acts 9:9—When Saul (who became Paul) was traumatized by the intense Christ Light while he was traveling on the road to Damascus in order to have the followers of the messianic imposter, Jesus/Jeshua of Nazareth, arrested and prosecuted, he became blind for three (3) days.

Acts 10:16—Peter's vision concerning the cleanliness of certain animals for human consumption was repeated three (3) times for emphasis and authenticity.

Revelation 9:17–18 (three very appropriate numbers here)—Three (3) plagues (fire, smoke and sulphur) destroyed one-third (3) of mankind in John's vision. (Note: It seems that Spirit subconsciously directed those who prepared the Holy Bible to apply the numbers 9, 17 and 18 for this frightening scenario because the number 9 pertains to the evolutionary process for soul perfection and destiny of humankind. The number 17 pertains to the necessary experience of suffering that can lead to redemption, while the number 18 refers to the time factor that is involved.)

Number Seven (7)

Since the number 7 is such a profound spiritual number and the basic number of God or Creative Forces, and also because it is so omnipresent in the first book (Genesis) and also the last book (Revelation) of the Holy Bible, it was cited and emphasized at the beginning of this chapter. However, the following list of incidents and examples that involve the number 7 are derived from other parts of the Holy Bible.

Matthew 18:21–22—When Peter asked Christ if he should forgive his brother or fellow man seven (7) times, he was told that he should do it seventy times seven. Also, did the number 70 (10 x 7) pertain to the 70 years mentioned in Jeremiah 25:11 and the 70 weeks cited in Daniel 9:24, both of which applied to God's completed purpose?

Matthew 14:17–21—Jesus/Jeshua metaphysically multiplies five loaves of bread and two fish (=7) to feed over five thousand men, women and children.

Mark 16:9—Verse 9 reveals that Christ previously had cast out (exorcized) seven (7) devils or demons from Mary of Magdala/Magdalene. (Incidentally, the internationally-popular, blasphemous book, The da Vinci Code, attempts to convince gullible readers that Jesus was married to this Mary, and that they even had a child together. What utter nonsense because Jesus/Jeshua had told the disciples that anyone devoting his life

44

to God should not marry, obviously because familial situations would manifest many disruptions and diversions for such a dedicated person. This is why Catholicism forbids its priests to marry, but the strong, irresistible sexual urge in human males is a serious prohibitive factor, which is woefully cited in the Edgar Cayce spiritual readings where it states that *sex* is the strongest force in man!

Deuteronomy 8:8 (double material number 8)—Regarding Moses and the promised land, God offers Israel seven (7) special foods, viz., wheat, barley, grapes (vines), figs, pomegranates, olives (for oil) and honey. Current scientific nutritional studies are proving the exceptional health value for all of these foods, especially purple and dark red grapes and pomegranates (most recent) for overall health and a strengthened immune system. The Edgar Cayce medical and health information that has benefited thousands of ill people advocated the ingestion of olive oil to enhance digestion of all consumed foods. The Cayce spiritual source also stated that Concord grapes (all purple and dark red grapes should be beneficial for this purpose), when ingested solely for a period of three (3) days, will detoxify a human body, and a small amount of olive oil should culminate the process. Drinking diluted Concord grape juice should facilitate the process. Indeed, a 2007 Italian study revealed that even melatonin (the sleep hormone regulator produced in the pineal endocrine gland, also called the "third eye" for meditation) was discovered in some varieties of purple grapes, and the resveratrol in purple grapes is considered almost a panacea for good health of a human body.

Gospels of Matthew, Luke and John (7 references)— Jesus/Jeshua spoke seven (7) times during His ordeal on the cross of crucifixion.

Complete Bible—Researchers and scholars have listed forty (testing number) different instances in the Holy Bible where the number 7 is mentioned concerning rituals, miracles, symbols, social customs and material items.

Number Nine (9)

As previously mentioned in the discussion for the number 3, the spirit of Jesus/Jeshua departed the physical body at the ninth (9) hour while on the cross with two other condemned victims (3 persons and 3 crosses that should be added to the number 3 discussion).

Perhaps the most enigmatic depiction of the number 9 is found at the end of the four gospels (see John 21:9-11) where the resurrected Christ appears to the disciples for the last time just prior to His Ascension, and it seems to be significant that there were only seven (emphasizing again the very spiritual number 7) disciples present at this final meeting with the Master. Having been out all night fishing, the disciples were thoroughly depressed and disillusioned from having lost their Messiah and incomparable spiritual Teacher, and this condition was compounded by having caught no fish. As the boat approached the lake shore, they saw a man who called out to them and told them to cast the fishnet at the *right* side of the boat, which instantly became filled with fish. Then John, who was the most attuned and in harmony with the mind of the Christ, recognized the helpful man as the Master, obviously via intuition and/or telepathy because the resurrected physical man, Jesus/Jeshua, was still undergoing the biological and chemical process of metamorphosing the Light body back into an atomic, third-dimensional form. This is why Mary Magdalene was unable to recognize her Teacher at the burial chamber, but only via His voice and Love.

After rushing to meet the resurrected Christ—He really was not Jesus/Jeshua the limited man any longer—they then dragged the filled net to shore, dumped out all the large fish and, quite strangely and irrationally, began to count all those fish while their beloved Master Teacher was standing there! The total amount of fish was the very odd number of 153. Why such an uneven, seemingly inconsequential, total number for this miraculous final act of Christ just prior to His Ascension? Of course, 1+5+3 equals the human destiny number 9, but why such an indirect presentation of this crucial number? However, when we associate the number 17 with the number 9, as always should be the case based on the human-eradicating Great Flood factor in Genesis, we can discern that the numbers 1 through 17 collectively add up to 153, and also that 9 x 17 revealingly equals the mysterious number 153! Here we should be reminded that the Christ advised, "Ask, and you will receive; seek, and you will find; knock, and it will be opened."

Other indirect references to the number 9 in the Holy Bible are:

Revelation 21:17—The wall of the new Jerusalem is 144 (9) cubits in height. Of course, this measurement number in this case is more concerned with the squaring of the number 12, which is the number of perfect structure. However, there are two factors that seem to be considered here because the number 144 vibrates to the human destiny number 9, as does the number 144,000 (1,000 x 144), which pertains to the total number of people in the 12 tribes of Israel (Rev. 7:4) and the special 144,000 disciplined male followers of Christ (Rev. 14:1–5).

Revelation 13:17 and 18 (three potent numbers)—The number of the "beast" (human ego and unmitigated will?) and a "man's name" is 666, which equals the *time* number 18, and this number reduces and vibrates to the number 9 for humankind.

47

Revelation 12:6—The symbolic woman was sustained in the wilderness for 1260 (9) days, which is a "half time" versus a "whole time" of 2520 (9) days/years in biblical time and cycles. Most or all of the Book of Revelation involves symbolism and allegory, and these time-cycle periods seem to apply to the Gentile period and Israel's punishment.

Luke 10:1—Jesus/Jeshua appointed 72 (9) of His followers to go on a healing mission. Similarly, spiritual sources have informed humankind that there are 72 (9) names of God and 144 (9) sacred expressions of God.

Number Twelve (12)

The number 12 in the Holy Bible is of utmost importance, beginning with the twelve (12) tribes of Israel and extending to the twelve (12) disciples of Christ and the measurement factor (12) in the *new* city of Jerusalem (Book of Revelation) with its twelve (12) gates. Since there are twelve (12) signs of the zodiac and their corresponding twelve (12) houses that pertain to the twelve (12) basic human personalities, it may be surmised that each of the disciples of Christ represented one of the personality signs of the zodiac in the spiritual science of astrology. Unfortunately and tragically, the vast majority of humankind still has no awareness and knowledge of the true nature, purpose and value of astrology and numerology that can be combined harmoniously to create a chart and "roadmap" that can direct the course of each entity's life in the earth plane. (Incidentally, the 25th day of December cannot possibly be the birth day of Jesus/ Jeshua of Nazareth because, astrologically, Sun in Capricorn pertains to the most materialistic time of each year that refers to business and world governments and their leaders, obviously indicating that this is the worst time to celebrate the birthday of the Saviour because it is always focused on ultimate greed whereby virtually all retail businesses expect to actualize about

25% of their profits for the year. So it is far more likely that the Christ Soul entered embodiment as Jesus/Jeshua with Sun in Pisces, the sign of the humanitarian that can lead eventually to *martyrdom*.)

Other specific references to the number 12 in the Holy Bible are:

Matthew 19:28—Jesus/Jeshua talks of the twelve (12) thrones in heaven where the twelve (12) disciples will sit to judge the twelve (12) tribes of Israel.

Matthew 26:53—At Gethsemane, when the soldiers came to arrest Jesus/Jeshua, Peter used his sword to protect Him, but Christ told Peter to put away his sword because He could summon twelve (12) legions of angels to protect Him. He then said that all those who live by the sword will perish by the sword. So why had Jesus/Jeshua previously instructed the disciples to procure and arm themselves with swords, and then later acquiescing to only the two swords that the disciples could acquire? Certainly, the reason could not have been merely to illustrate the law of cause-and-effect (karma). It seems much more likely that the Master Soul was testing their faith in Him and His omnipotent power that He had demonstrated so many times for all of the disciples. Therefore, instead of obsequiously complying with His instruction to obtain swords, they should have reminded Him of His awesome power and also that the Ten Commandments that were given to Moses on Mount Sinai/ Horeb forbid the killing of another human being.

John 11:9—Jesus/Jeshua refers to the twelve (12) hours of a day and the importance of *light* versus *darkness*, obviously referring to the spiritual and satanic realms and conditions.

Luke 2:42—As mentioned previously, Jesus/Jeshua was twelve (12) years old when He began to practice the Christ philosophy and ministry regarding His questioning and teaching as applied to the Jewish religious leaders. When scolded by His parents, He responded, "Don't you know that I must be about my Father's business?" Indeed, the Edgar Cayce spiritual source revealed that Jesus/Jeshua, being the Christ Soul, was conscious of His ultimate mission for humankind from when He had been in the earth plane as Adam! So Jesus/Jeshua obviously was trying to impart this truth to all human beings when He referred to Himself as the "Son of man."

Actually, the Cayce spiritual source went much farther back in time regarding the purpose and mission of the Christ Soul by revealing that this first perfected Master Soul first entered physical embodiment in the great *continent* of Atlantis that existed at the present location of the Atlantic Ocean, as this name certainly implies. However, at that time many thousands of years ago, the souls entering the material earth plane, and being in their normal etheric form, still retained the capability to both enter and exit the physical bodies of the "proanthropoids" and other animals and material forms as a unique experience. Having become too preoccupied and lost in matter, a Divine Plan was initiated whereby the Christ Soul would enter embodiment as Amelius to guide the errant souls through an evolutionary process to accomplish *soul perfection* that apparently would culminate in a future Christ Soul incarnation as Adam to begin the special Adamic race, and finally as Jesus/Jeshua of Nazareth. This last incarnation required His physical martyrdom to demonstrate that all human beings must eventually crucify the Ego and attune their will to the Will of their Creator by becoming LOVE individualized. Hence, this complete scenario indicates that both the Creationists and Evolutionists are partially correct in their beliefs and philosophy.

Number Thirteen (13)

The number 13 is really a very spiritual number because Jesus/Jeshua and the specially-chosen twelve disciples combined to form a powerful spiritual group of 13 entities. This potent spiritual aspect was later applied to the thirteen (13) American colonies that initiated the greatest world democratic experiment since the incubation of democracy in Greece. Perhaps it was because of the great power of the number 13 that eventually fear became attached to it even to the point of superstition that obviously resulted in the invention of the very polysyllabic word, *triskaidekaphobia,* that certainly applies to many uneducated and unenlightened people in the world.

Number Seventeen (17)

Actually, an entire book could be written about all the examples and ramifications of the number 17 because of its pervasiveness and importance concerning the spiritual evolution and process of perfection for all souls in embodiment in any and all incarnations/lifetimes in the material earth plane. The crucial number 17 was initially cited and discussed in Chapter 2 and then in this chapter regarding the massive, human-annihilating Flood, and also its veiled involvement with the number 153 regarding the total number of fish that the resurrected Jesus/Jeshua had manifested inside the fishnet for the seven disciples at their final meeting just prior to Christ's Ascension (John 21:9–11). It is always involved with either *suffering* or *redemption,* or simply involved with human activities in the earth plane because the numbers 1 and 7 vibrate to the very material number 8. The number 17 also was discussed during the discourse for the number 9 in this chapter, so the close relationship to the human destiny number 9 should be apparent. To reiterate the reason for the selection by Spirit of the anomalous number 17 (versus 3, 6, 9, 18 and 27), the seemingly most plausible purpose may have involved the combination of the human destiny number 9 and the most material number 8, and these two number vibrations coalesce to create the vibratory rate and power of the number 17. These last three numbers—3 is the *whole* number—indicate that the spiritual soul in a human body only can be perfected via numerous sojourns in the material earth plane, as the Edgar Cayce spiritual source revealed and explained quite thoroughly. The succeeding chapters of this book should tend to illustrate and prove the omnipresence and full purpose of the number 17 in the affairs of humankind, and its association with some of the world's great mysteries, such as the existence and purpose of the Great Pyramid in Egypt and the *real* spiritual meaning of the Pythagorean Divine Triangle as the Life Theorem.

Regarding other direct and indirect references to the number 17 in the Holy Bible, in Genesis 17(!), God makes a covenant with Abram (still not Abraham) concerning his designated role as the *father* of many nations. Then God strangely changes Abram's name to Abraham, perhaps because the name Abram vibrates to the number 17 (1+2+9+1+4). The name *Abraham* has an *h* (8) added and another *a* (1), which, when combined, add another 9 vibration that results in the collective number 26 vibration that reduces and vibrates to the number 8 of materiality and the earth plane. Moreover, the number 26 seems to have an affinity with the overall concept and evolutionary process regarding humankind, and this is further indicated in the hypotenuse (spirit/soul) of the Pythagorean Divine Triangle when it is *wholistically* interpreted (see Chapter 6). Of course, the basic number 8 is the ideal vibrational energy regarding Abraham's new mission and destiny as the patriarch of many nations.

Also in Genesis 17(!), God even changes the name of Abram's/Abraham's wife, Sarai, to Sarah, and the letter *i* (9) becomes an *h* (8), the same letter that was added to Abram's name. Of course, the Hebrew cabala/kabala and its mysticism, as well as original languages and sounds, have to be applied and evaluated in this matter when attempting to interpret and assign meanings to all ancient practices, activities and mysteries.

Since the name, *God*, vibrates to the number 17 (7+6+4), it appears that humankind invented and applied this word for its Creator because so many people associate God with duty, coercion and suffering, especially regarding the contest of *wills*. However, the word, *man*, vibrates to the number 10(4+1+5), which, when combined with the God vibration of 17, results in the potent number 27 that is a *triplication* of the human destiny number 9. Moreover, the 10 is the number of the perfected Soul.

Perhaps the best way to conclude this discussion of the number 17 is to refer to the scenario depicted in Chapter 17(!) of the Gospel of John wherein Jesus/Jeshua utters His lengthy prayer concerning His disciples and the imminent completion of His earthly mission for humankind. In Verse 17(!), He speaks of the importance of Truth. Apparently, His long prayer is so important for all of humankind that the Edgar Cayce spiritual source advised everyone to read and study the fourteenth through seventeenth (14–17) chapters of the Gospel of John and to realize and *believe* that Christ was/is speaking to every human being/entity who has ever experienced a sojourn/lifetime on planet Earth.

Number Eighteen (18)

The number 18 is best cited and emphasized (albeit indirectly) in the Holy Bible where the number 666 appears in the Book of Revelation. This perplexing, enigmatic number is introduced in Chapter 13, Verse 18, which the reader should notice are two very significant and appropriate numbers. This very symbolic, triple-digit number pertains to the "beast" (man's ego and lower nature?) and a "man's name" and the triplicated number 6 vibrates to the *time* number 18, which is twice the cyclic number 9. Since Verse 17 of Chapter 13 refers to buying and selling, it could be presumed that the amount of gold (666 talents) that King Solomon received annually (see I Kings 10:14–15) is somehow related to this number in Revelation.

Another possible correlation to the number 666 can be found in the Edgar Cayce spiritual information wherein the prophetic year of 1998 (= 27, number of big endings) is referred to as the culminating year of the predicted 40-year (1958–1998) "testing period" for humankind. This special year of 1998 is the product of the triplication of the number 666 (3 x 666 = 1998). A major astrological event occurred in 1998 when the *spiritual* planet, Neptune, entered the zodiacal sign of Aquarius, which is associated with the "New Age" that even Jesus/Jeshua referred to as a special time marker for humankind. Moreover, Aquarius is the sign of humanitarianism (more mentally than physically, as would be the case for its adjoining zodiacal sign of Pisces), and the prophetic Mayan Sacred Calendar/Tzolkin indicates that by the year 2012 all human beings should have learned to cease their stupid, wasteful wars and learned to live in peace, harmony and love with one another. This seems totally incredulous and ludicrous until we contemplate the scenario of the so-called *rapture* (see Matthew 24:40 prophecy). When Christ said that some people would be "taken" and that some people would be "left", apparently only those who will have learned to manifest and apply unconditional love to their fellow human beings by perhaps 2011 (see Chapter 5) will be "taken" via a dematerialization or decorporation of the physical body and transfigured into a "Whole Light Being", such as Dr. James

J. Hurtak depicts in his profoundly spiritual book, The Book of Knowledge: The Keys of Enoch.

Two other factors could materialize before 2011 or 2012 that quickly would induce humankind to cease its aggressiveness, belligerence and materialism. A huge asteroid or comet could veer toward a collision course with Earth, or even extraterrestrial beings, benevolent or malevolent, could make widespread or global contact with humankind instead of the merely individual contacts that have been reported throughout the world. Dr. Hurtak speaks of the very benevolent "*ultra*terrestrials."

Referring again to the beginning transit of Neptune in Aquarius in 1998 (3 x 666), coincidentally and quite synchronistically, Neptune will complete its transit of this humanitarian, revolutionary, New Age sign in 2012, which is the calculated and predicted prophetic culminating year of the Mayan Sacred Calendar/Tzolkin. The indication from various spiritual sources is that in late (winter solstice) 2012, all of the fully-spiritualized human beings will be metamorphosed into fifth-(5 is the *number* of man)dimensional "Light beings" as part of the new "fifth root race" that even the Edgar Cayce spiritual source had mentioned way back in the early 1930s.

Regarding the "buying and selling" mentioned in Verse 17 of Chapter 13 in Revelation and the associated number 666 and its triplication to 1998, in this year the global financial system nearly collapsed when Russia defaulted on its debt and some Asian countries nearly entered bankruptcy. Also, the American huge hedge fund, Long-Term Capital Management, went bankrupt, causing stock and bond markets to plunge. As usual, typically soft-hearted Pisces Alan Greenspan, the U.S. Federal Reserve Chairman, quickly printed enough fiat dollars to "paper-over" the crisis, but now in 2008 this band-aid remedy truly will not work effectively and safely any longer because of the interconnectedness of the global financial system. So perhaps the number 666 in the final book of the Holy Bible is indicating that a global financial calamity will occur in the near future (think *derivatives*).

Number Twenty-Four (24)

The number 24 appears in Chapter 4 of Revelation wherein it pertains to the opening of the sealed book and the associated twenty-four (24) elders and their twenty-four (24) thrones.

Regarding the present appalling spiritual condition of humankind, it would seem that the most pertinent reference to the number 24 in the Holy Bible can be found in Chapter 24 of the Gospel of Matthew, wherein Jesus/Jeshua delineated the frightening prophecy that everyone in the world, regardless of their religion, should be reading, studying and meditating upon quite often, especially when considering the present global sociological and material conditions. Besides the man-made horror of the terrorist destruction of the World Trade Towers in New York City, two recent applicable severe global events were the gigantic submarine earthquake near Indonesia that generated a huge tsunami, causing innumerable human deaths, and the massive hurricane that devastated the coastal region of southeastern America. The Asian earthquake-tsunami occurred on December 26, 2004, and the collective numerals of this date (1-2-2-6-2-0-0-4) vibrate to the number 17 of suffering. Also, the original evening news report in America stated that the Richter Scale magnitude was 8.9 (= 17), but this number was changed the next day to 9.0, and both numbers pertain to the suffering of the 17 and the human destiny number 9 and the spiritual evolutionary process of humankind. Moreover, astrologically, Uranus, the planet of surprise changes, was still transiting (2003-2011) the zodiacal *water* sign of Pisces, which is the assigned sign and symbol of suffering. So it seems evident that these two ocean-originating disasters had a direct correlation with this astrological scenario.

At this point, we might contemplate exactly what Christ meant in Matthew 24 when He spoke of the "birth pangs of the New Age." Certainly, we may expect these catastrophes to continue and even exacerbate, especially until at least 2011, if the prophecies of the Mayan calendar and the general scenario of the three outer *consciousness* planets, Uranus, Neptune and Pluto, prove to be correct. To be more specific, Dr. Carl Johan Calleman's very *spiritual* interpretation of the Mayan calendar reveals that there are nine (9) Creation Cycles, and the last Cycle begins on February 11, 2011, and ends on October 28, 2011. Since 9 is the human cyclic number and also the number of endings, it seems quite appropriate that the ninth (9) and last spiritual evolutionary cycle should comprise only a short 9-month period, just as a human being is fully created during a 9-month gestation period.

The overall Christ prophecy in Matthew 24 obviously has been completed for the earthly and human conditions, but the scenario involving the moon and the sun illumination conditions has yet to manifest. Of course, a few gigantic volcanic eruptions, like Krakatoa, should accommodate this part of the prophecy. The magnitude of the *celestial* events of Matthew 24 may be manifesting now, as both the Fatima Prophecy and Dr. James J. Hurtak's spiritually-guided information frightfully predict and that he has presented for humankind in The Book of Knowledge: The keys of Enoch. We need only to contemplate and evaluate extant global conditions, and further realize that the presence of more that six billion—yes, that's 6,000,000,000!—souls are now inhabiting human bodies. Hence, we may assume that, at the soul or *superconscious* level of consciousness, many of us suspect or even *know* that something BIG is soon to happen.

Moreover, the Cayce spiritual information suggests to this author that some of these souls may have come from "other systems" in the universe(s) solely to experience this final phase of the spiritual evolutionary process for *all* souls that were a part of the *original* Creation. Perhaps this factor may assist some of those individuals who cannot accept and believe the concept and reality of reincarnation, albeit its associated law of cause-and-effect (karma) should make perfect sense and justice to any human being.

Number Twenty-Seven (27)

The number 27 is perhaps most prominently noted for the Holy Bible when we learn and realize that there are 27 canonical books of the most important section of the Holy Bible, which is the New Testament. Indeed, the four separate accounts of Jesus/Jeshua and His Christine Ministry should be sufficient to convince any human being that this most definitely was and is the promised Messiah, especially if the seeker of Truth invites the Christ Spirit to permeate his/her full consciousness. Additionally or alternatively, even a cursory study of the vast, detailed Edgar Cayce spiritual information regarding the numerous earthly incarnations, both physically and metaphysically, of the Christ Soul can be very persuasive regarding the veracity of the information.

Whereas the New Testament primarily involves the "new covenant" that Christ presented for humankind, the Old Testament is basically a *history* of the innumerable instances in which the strong will of the Jewish people continually attempted to circumvent or even supersede the will of Jehovah, which merely elicited and manifested more suffering for themselves. Obviously, like most humans even today, they never really recognized and understood the immutable law of cause-and-effect that Christ later defined so plainly by warning that we reap what we sow, even if it is postponed until a future lifetime because no one can impudently mock God without the dire consequences that will become mandatory to restore a karmic balance.

Even at the very beginning of the Holy Bible, in Genesis 8:14, the number 27 is particularly mentioned as the final day when Noah and his family were told by God to leave the long suffering of their miserable ordeal on that great ship that must have been overloaded with so many pairs of animals and birds. Hence, even here in this condition and scenario it is evident that the number 27, being the triplication of the cyclic number 9, definitely pertains to a time of endings in a big way. [Incidentally, when we apply the biblical 30-day period for each month, it reveals that the normal gestation period to create a human being is 270 (27 with a cipher) days, which is 9 biblical months of 30 days each. Therefore, the biblical solar year contained 360 (9) days. The change to 365.242 days for our present solar year obviously occurred when, as the Edgar Cayce spiritual information indicates, a large planet, located between Mars and Jupiter, exploded, thereby resulting in the countless asteroids that now orbit the sun in that zone of our solar system. Isaiah 13:13 (the potent spiritual number duplicated) appears to be a verbatim confirmation of this scenario for our solar system and Earth's present position in relationship to our sun.]

Number Thirty-Three (33)

Biblical scholars have accepted the earthly life of Jesus/ Jeshua of Nazareth as having spanned thirty-three (33) years, and this is corroborated by the Fatima Prophecy information that is presented in Chapter 7 of this book. Since the number 33 is the third master number in the spiritual science of numerology that pertains to great *responsibility* and *adjustments*, it is obvious why the Christ Soul was given 33 years to prepare for and to complete His messianic mission for humankind and to teach and illustrate all of the prerequisite information and spiritual knowledge that would act as the catalyst for awakening our soul and consciousness to the full awareness of who we really are and why we must experience and endure the vicissitudes of each incarnation/lifetime in the material earth plane.

Number Forty (40)

As noted at the beginning of this chapter regarding the great soul-cleansing Flood and Noah's long ark ordeal, and even continuing to the testing of Jesus/Jeshua by Satan right after John had baptized Him, it certainly is obvious that 40 is the primary *testing* number throughout the Holy Bible.

In Genesis 15:13, God tells Abram (not yet Abraham) that the Hebrew people will spend 400 (10 x 40) years in captivity in a strange land (Egypt).

In Jonah 3:4, the prophet Jonah enters the wicked city of Nineveh and tells the people that the city will be destroyed in forty (40) days if the inhabitants do not change their lifestyle.

In Matthew 4:2, Jesus/Jeshua fasts for forty (40) days and nights during Satan's temptation.

In Numbers 14:33, God tells Moses that his corrupt people will be made to wander in the desert for forty (40) years.

In Exodus 24:18, Moses was on Mount Sinai (Horeb) for forty (40) days and nights while receiving the Ten Commandments. Even Elijah, who later would be reincarnated as John the Baptist according to Jesus/Jeshua, also will spend forty (40) days and nights on this mountain (I Kings 19:8).

60

In Acts 1:3, we learn that Jesus/Jeshua had appeared to His disciples (three times) during a 40-day period following His resurrection.

Numbers One Hundred Fifty-Three (153) and Six Hundred Sixty-Six (666)

These two very important and significant symbolic numbers have been explored and evaluated in the preceding discussions of the numbers 9 and 18, respectively.

Number Sixteen Hundred (1600)

This unusual number is mentioned in Revelation 14:20 as a unit of measurement, but it may have other ramifications that are examined in Chapter 8 (the very material number) that pertains to the evolution of the United States of America, specifically alluding to the assigned number of the White House that is located at 1600 Pennsylvania Avenue in Washington, D.C. The fact that this number is a product of forty times the testing number (40 x 40 = 1600) certainly applies to a long period of severe testing.

CHAPTER 4

The Great Pyramid and its Numbers of Revelation for Humankind

If pyramidologists would read and study the Edgar Cayce psychically-obtained information regarding the purpose, time and method of construction, and especially its real architect, they would receive a complete understanding of the Great Pyramid at the Giza plateau in Egypt. It had a very special spiritual purpose for having been built during the period from 10,490 to 10,390 B.C. (not B.C.E. because Christ is the true reference for chronology or calendrical time). Etymologically, the word *pyramid* has various derivations, but the very obvious definition informs us that *pyr* means fire and *amid* means middle, which combine to mean fire-in-the-middle! This definition appears nonsensical and ludicrous until we look at a small replica (made of any material) of the Great Pyramid that is placed under the influence and exposure of Kirlian photography that involves static electricity (see Figure 1). The glowing beam of energy, that researchers have termed "biocosmic energy", is concentrated at the apex of the pyramid, and research by Dr. G. Patrick Flanagan in the early1970s culminated with the publication of his detailed book, Pyramid Power. At least two pyramidologists have determined that the beam of etheric energy is focused at the level of the so-called King's Chamber, which is an artificial name that undoubtedly was designated by certain pyramidologists who were ignorant of the true history of this magnificent structure and its very meaningful dimensions. Based on Kirlian electrical photography and extensive investigative research by Dr. Flanagan, it appears that the pyramid configuration is the perfect focusing device for the pre-matter substance called *ether*, and a tested spiritual source informed some spiritual seekers that three-dimensional, atomic matter is merely a form of *compacted ether*, which is subatomic and also referred to as the *fourth* state of matter. (Incidentally, Dr. Flanagan stated that the Ark of the Covenant that God told Moses to construct was essentially a large electric capacitor that functioned via static electricity and stored from 600 to 1,000 volts, and also that this container for the Ten Commandments had the same dimensions as the so-called coffer in the King's Chamber of the Great Pyramid.)

While in a self-induced altered state of consciousness, the authenticated Edgar Cayce was asked to reveal details about the Great Pyramid concerning its designer/architect and method of construction. The spiritual source replied, ".....by those forces of nature as make for iron to swim. Stone floats in the air in the same manner" (buoyancy and levitation/antigravity, respectively). The Cayce source also indicated that the architect was Hermes (Thoth Hermes Trismegistus), and this is corroborated quite emphatically and convincingly in Manly P. Hall's mammoth, masterful treatise on metaphysics that was assigned the audacious title, The Secret Teachings of All Ages. Both of these very sincere, dedicated spiritual sources also indicated that Hermes (his common name) was one of the very timely incarnations of the Christ Soul, and also that one of the principal *material* reasons for the construction of the Great Pyramid was to reflect the change (following the explosion of a planet that had been positioned between Mars and Jupiter— think *asteroids*) of Earth's solar year from the original, biblical 360 days to the imperfect present 365.242 days. Moreover, the internal design and structure of the Great Pyramid was intended for those spiritual adepts who were completing their final degrees (to number 33?) concerning Mastership (called the Great White Brotherhood—no racial connotation)

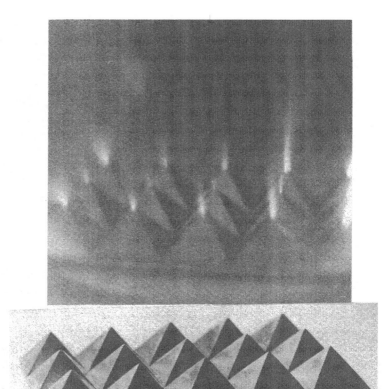

This small (3" x 5") pyramid matrix, called the Pyramid Energy Generator, is an early 1970 invention and result of a serious, extensive study of models of the Great Pyramid in Egypt by G. Patrick Flanagan, Ph.D. The variations in intensity of the "bioplasma" beams of concentrated etheric energy are directly related to the sharpness of the apex of each of the epoxy pyramids.

FIGURE 1: Kirlian electrical photograph of a pyramid energy grid (PEG) illustrating pyramid power

and the Cayce source added that Jesus/Jeshua and John (later called "the Baptist") had completed the "last of their Brotherhood degrees" in the Great Pyramid.

As to the real age of the Great Pyramid as being about 12,000 years old, the Cayce source revealed that the enigmatic Sphinx is even older, as recent archeological and scientific investigations are confirming, especially by establishing that the erosion at the excavated base of the Sphinx was caused by *water* before the present desert was formed. Surprisingly, computer analysis indicates that the pharaoh-like head and headdress is not correctly proportioned to the rest of the Sphinx, so a pharoah may have reduced an original larger head to satisfy his ego and assume credit for the construction and purpose of the Sphinx. Of course, it could be that this was the original headdress that later Egyptian pharaohs merely copied from the possibly earlier Atlantean refugee builders. Since many sphinx artifacts have been discovered that contain the head of a woman, it is plausible to postulate that the original design of the Sphinx, having a woman's head, was intended to illustrate both the masculine and feminine genders of human beings. Indeed, the Greek Sphinx, whose riddle anyone was invited to solve, had a female head on a lion's body. However, quite logically, there also were two breasts of the female, indicating that the Giza Sphinx also may have had breasts where the frontal section has been severely eroded. (Incidentally, it should be pertinent for the theme of this book that the number 9 vibration results from the numbers 4, 2 and 3 that comprised the riddle of the Greek Sphinx.)

Having mentioned that the Cayce spiritual source stated that Atlantean refugees journeyed to the present Egyptian land area and most likely built the Sphinx, the Cayce source also revealed that these people also left records that prove the existence of Atlantis and their history and these documents are entombed in three places in the earth. The one in Egypt is located near the right forepaw of the Sphinx, where current ground-penetrating radar is being utilized to detect this chamber. However, it is very unlikely that this method will be successful because the Cayce source said that this records chamber has a pyramidal shape, which would not provide the required reflective surface for the probing medium, and this also includes low-frequency sound waves. Incidentally, it should be mentioned here that these detection methods recently have located more hidden cavities/chambers in the Great Pyramid.

In Dr. James J. Hurtak's highly-technical book of spiritual science, The Book of Knowledge: The Keys of Enoch, he refers to the Great Pyramid as a "geophysical and astrophysical computer" that the Holy Bible portrays as an "altar to God" (Isaiah 19:19).

Albeit the present inhabitants of Egypt intensely want the rest of the world's human denizens to accept and believe that they were the designers and builders of both the Great Pyramid and Sphinx, the Cayce source, while viewing the Akashic Record or Book of Life, revealed that Atlantean refugees (as stated above) had migrated to northern Africa way back when the Nile River flowed in the *opposite* direction. This geological oddity can be readily understood when the Cayce readings are read and studied concerning "pole shifts" and tectonic plate movements. Since the "red race" of the five human races had originated in Atlantis, according to the Cayce source, the present day Egyptians do not conform to this condition, but they may be the result of miscegenation, just as many people are today in the world.

Perhaps the most astounding commentary regarding the purpose and meaning of the Great Pyramid can be found in Key 1-0-8 (= 9 and an 18) of Dr. Hurtak's profoundly-revelatory book that was mentioned above. Here it is revealed that one primary reason for the existence of the Great Pyramid is to "instruct man in the awesome and regenerating architecture of cataclysmic geology." Perhaps this perplexing, complicated, scientific statement may be related to the "powerful generators" that are mentioned in the last paragraph of this chapter. The installers of these subterranean generators also said that their main purpose was to "help eliminate an alarming degree of axial excursion at the north and south poles" of Earth.

Concerning the specific numbers of the Great Pyramid and their spiritual purpose, the most important number of this "Bible in stone" is what pyramidologists call the "displacement factor" of 286.1 pyramid inches that vibrate to the number 17 (2+8+6+1) of *suffering* and *redemption*, which appears to be the main theme of this mysterious edifice. It seems obvious to this author that there is a direct correspondence between the number 17 vibration of the Great Pyramid and the number 17 that is associated with the Great Flood in the Holy Bible, which further indicates that the Christ Soul, as Hermes, really had been the architect of this "Bible in stone." While the so-called Queen's Chamber is located at the centerline of the vertical axis of the Great Pyramid, the King's Chamber is strangely offset by 286.1 pyramid inches (a pyramid inch is merely .001 thousandths more than an English inch). From the intersection of the floor line to the first low passageway to where the "Time Line" enters the north wall of the King's Chamber, there are 286.1 (17) pyramid inches. Pyramidologist Howard B. Rand long ago stated that this "displacement factor" is continuously found to be operating in various physical, spiritual and historical applications in such a manner as to witness to the work, divinity and atoning sacrifice of Jesus/Jeshua the Christ! Supporting and emphasizing the number 17 vibration of the Great Pyramid is the fact that the projected (i.e., including the now missing capstone) geometric height of the Pyramid is 5813 (= 17) pyramid inches. Most pyramidologists assume that the capstone for this truncated pyramidal structure had never been installed because it symbolically represents the Christ as the Saviour of humankind or this Adamic race. However, the Edgar Cayce spiritual source said that the capstone had been placed on the Great Pyramid and that it was "sounded" in some way to call the "initiates" to prayer, and many would gather around this spiritual edifice/altar. The Cayce source continued to say that the capstone was constructed of "brass, copper and gold", and the gold probably was in the form of a bright, shiny outer layer. When considering the common human traits of avarice and desire, it becomes apparent about what really happened to the precious capstone, and also the white marble (?) blocks that formed the Pyramid's façade. From a structural standpoint, the reason that pyramidologists assume that the capstone was not installed is because the perimeter at the base where it would be placed is "short by 286.1 inches and is principally due to this error [?] factor that was designed into the base of the Great Pyramid itself." Additionally, this key value of 286.1 is found also where the ceiling of the Grand Gallery is 286.1 pyramid inches higher than its ascending passageway.

This author's friend, the late pyramidologist and general metaphysician, Raymond Ouellette, said that the number 286.1 is the "main factor in the reconciliation scheme of all things" while he was pondering the suffering and redemption theme of the Great Pyramid. Even the accepted primary pyramidologist, David Davidson, was so impressed with this so-called displacement factor that he wrote: "This factor is of such transcendant value that it operates throughout [the Pyramid] in a manner wholly beyond the ingenuity of the human mind to devise." Again, we can see that the Christ Soul *had* to be the architect of the Great Pyramid or "Bible in stone." Raymond Ouellette wrote that this value of 286.1 is very necessary as a basis for calculation in astronomy, and also that the entire systems of symbology and chronology would be useless without this displacement factor. Indeed, Mr. Ouellette went so far as to say that the distance to our sun, the sidereal and anomalistic years, the precessional cycles, ellipticals and gravitational values, including the variations and eccentricities of the orbit itself, would be impossible of demonstration without the calculative system of the Great Pyramid, which again points to the Christ Soul as the Instrument that God/Creative Forces used to present this Bible in stone to humankind.

To summarize the foregoing information, comments and interpretations, it would seem that God's intention for both the specific and general purpose of the Great Pyramid is for humankind to awaken, realize and acknowledge that this displacement factor symbolizes the soul's sinful error and misalignment of its will (birthright) from the Will of its Creator or First Cause. Hence, if a soul resides in a physical body long enough—it may require many lifetimes—it should come to realize that it will learn best via a mandatory degree of *suffering*, and that such suffering may be averted in a series of incarnations only to be all concentrated in one specific lifetime based on the amount of negative karma that may have accumulated. This, simply, is the law of cause-and-effect that applies to everyone.

To reinforce the purpose and meaning of the number 17 in the Great Pyramid, the dramatic chronological ending date was calculated to have been September 17, 2001, and hopefully this time the number 17 corresponded to the 17th day of the month when Noah's ark mercifully grounded on the mountain in Ararat, signifying *redemption* for humankind because God/Creative Forces certainly is fully aware of how many times that His (intended) companion Souls have experienced the lessons of the material earth plane. However, the last day of the chronological ending date was not on the 27th day of a month, signifying a final ending, so we can surmise that the big ending has yet to ensue—

perhaps in 2012? As a possible parallel, we need to consider the time period between when the water had receded, leaving dry land, and when Noah and his family finally were permitted to exit that miserable ship on the 27th day of a month, which was a testing period of almost two months! Perhaps this last period of about two months corresponds to the relatively short period from September 17, 2001, to December 21, 2012, assuming that the chronology of the Mayan Sacred Calendar/Tzolkin has been correctly interpreted. Moreover, the other spiritual sources that have been mentioned, along with numerology and astrology, indicate that some profound, momentous changes will be occurring for humankind during the imminent years of 2011 and 2012.

Since 2001 for the Great Pyramid obviously was such a climactic year concerning the evolutionary process of humankind, it may be importantly synchronistic that the Cayce spiritual source predicted that a crucial global "pole shift" would occur during the period 2000–2001. Most, or even all, of the members of the Edgar Cayce Foundation's Association for Research and Enlightenment (including this author) presumed or assumed that the Cayce source was referring to a catastrophic geologic shifting of the earth's two poles. Since no physical global pole shift has occurred as of 2008, a reappraisal of the prediction is mandatory. Since Edgar Cayce was a very spiritual, sincere, altruistic human being, which was greatly augmented by his humanitarian, intuitive Pisces basic personality, perhaps Cayce was intuiting a shifting of consciousness between the two "poles" or hemispheres of all human brains and perhaps even referring to the two hemispheres of the global world. Indeed, the Cayce source cautioned that *every* thought that a person manifests in the brain/mind affects all human beings everywhere, and this is called the "collective unconscious." Hence, the Cayce source may have issued an accurate prediction at the time, but the collective prayers of the thousands of A.R.E. spiritualized members may have altered the course of cataclysmic geologic history.

To support the foregoing hypothesis, Dr. Carl Johan Calleman's seemingly very spiritual interpretation of the Mayan Sacred Calendar, especially concerning its central theme and focus on the number 9 as it applies to the spiritual evolutionary process of humankind, reveals that at this crucial time of the process the consciousness of all human beings is being altered, and for some people completely reversed, as manifested by the reversal of the "World Tree" that corresponds to the two hemispheres of both the world and the human brain. As stated above, this may accommodate the Cayce prediction regarding a "pole shift." This alteration and transformation of global human consciousness would have been augmented considerably by the long transit of Pluto (consciousness and transformation) in the zodiacal sign of Sagittarius (philosophy, religion and higher education) from 1995 until early 2008, and this is when there was a proliferation of "New Age" literature in the world. Moreover, the continuing (since early 2003) transit of Uranus (revolution and change) in the spiritual water sign of Pisces should be affecting human consciousness concerning humanitarianism and sacrifice. (Incidentally, the new, lengthy transit of Pluto in Capricorn that began in late January, 2008, should engender a global transformation in big business and in world governments and their leaders, and these changes could be severe in either a positive (expansive) or negative (excessive) way because giant Jupiter is activating the business sign of Capricorn during all of 2008.)

Other very significant, time-oriented numbers and measurements in the Great Pyramid are as follows:

1. The Grand Gallery is 1881 (equals the *time* number

71

18) pyramid inches long at the ceiling.

2. The location of the "coffer" or "open tomb" in the King's Chamber reflects the number 17 because the north, south and west sides of this enigmatic object are each at a distance of 58.13 (= 17) pyramid inches from the walls of the King's Chamber.

3. The length of the second low passageway leading to the King's Chamber is 153(!) pyramid inches, and the time period for the two low passageways on either side of the Antechamber is 153 months. Remember, this is the number of fish that Christ manifested in the fishnet of the seven disciples during their last meeting together after His resurrection and just prior to His ascension, and, of course, 9 x 17, and also the numerals 1 through 17, equal 153!

4. Regarding the Antechamber itself, the diagonal distance from its center to each of the four corners is 66.6 pyramid inches, which undoubtedly refers to the number 666 of the "beast" (man's lower nature, especially the strong sexual urge) in the Book of Revelation.

5. The angle of the passageways is 26 degrees, 18 minutes and 10 seconds (2+6+1+8+1+0 = 18, which again is the *time* number).

6. The Great Pyramid covers 13 (Christ with the 12 disciples) square acres.

7. The floor or base of the King's Chamber is vertically located at the fiftieth (50) course of masonry or blocks. As previously discussed in Chapter 2, the number 50 is called the Pythagorean Sacred Number because it is the total number for all three *squared* sides of the Divine Triangle (Life Theorem).

8. The constant, ambient temperature in the King's Chamber is 68 degrees, which is considered to be the ideal temperature for the human body concerning

longevity. Also, this number adds to 14, which reduces to 5, which is the *number* of man, whereas 9 is the cycle of man.

Concerning some specific prophetic dates in the 6,000-year chronology of the Great Pyramid, as derived via the agreed upon dating system, the following list is submitted:

1844 (= 17)—This year is very important because it falls precisely on the central axis of the Great Pyramid, and it corresponds exactly with the precessional cycle of 25,827 years.

1917 (= 18)—This was the year that the United States of America entered World War I and the Fatima "secret message" (later transcribed as a letter for the Vatican) was presented to three children during a Marian apparition and vision in Portugal.

1953 (= 18)—This is the year of the ending of the Great Step at the south wall of the King's Chamber, and it also was the year of the ending of the Korean War that involved the three communist countries of North Korea, China (mostly) and Russia (Soviet Union) versus the West (United Nations forces).

1998 (= 27)—Chronologically progressing, the "coffer" or "open tomb" is reached in the King's Chamber. This also was the final year of the 40-year "testing period" (1958–1998) that was cited in the Edgar Cayce spiritual information. Moreover, as mentioned previously, the number 1998 is the all-important triplication of the number 666 found in the Book of Revelation in the Holy Bible.

According to the chronological chart that was created by the renowned pyramidologist, David Davidson, the time period for the so-called Queen's Chamber is 17 years (1901–1918), and the period from the center of this same Chamber is 27 years (1909–1936) to the King's Chamber, and the time period for the King's Chamber (1936–1953) is again 17 years. Still progressing chronologically, the time period from the King's Chamber (1953) to September 17, 1986 (end of the 70th Jubilee), is 33 years, which is the Christ number and the highest degree in Freemasonry, as well as the total number of vertebrae in the human spinal column at birth (the sacral bone-fusion occurs later). Moreover, the combined period from 1936 to 1986 is the highly-spiritual number of 50 years. It should be noted that the September 17th day of 1986 above is the same as the number 17 day in the month of September in 2001 that concludes the 6,000-year time period of the Great Pyramid. The Seventh Millenary thus began on September 17, 2001, so this seventh (7 is the prime spiritual number and a key number for God/Creative Forces) 1,000-year period should be a very spiritual time, and it begins on the Hebrew Feast of Trumpets, according to a biblical scholar.

There are numerous other specific and significant numbers and time periods involved in the full chronology of the Great Pyramid, but this chapter is concerned primarily with a unifying synthesis regarding the revelatory numbers of the Holy Bible and other spiritual sources and mysteries.

Normally, this discourse on the Great Period now would be concluded by this author, but since the UFO (unidentified flying object) phenomenon is so globally pervasive and seemingly omnipresent, an inclusion of the following story and incredulous experience may pique the reader's interest and contemplation. Actually, the primary reason for adding this unique adventure to this discussion of the Great Pyramid can be attributed to its central theme that is associated with the number 9 destiny of humankind.

This amazing, astounding—but not altogether preposterous—scenario concerning the Great Pyramid began when United States Air Force member, Richard Miller, was assigned to Project Bluebook that the U.S.A.F. had initiated to investigate the inception of the epidemic of internationally-observed unidentified flying objects (UFOs) that Americans logically had named "flying saucers." Following his discharge from military service, the U.S.A.F. employed Miller as a roving UFO investigator, perhaps because he had been involved with the investigation of the January 7, 1948, incident in which a UFO appeared in the restricted air space above Fort Knox, Kentucky (where the *remnants* of U.S. gold are stored), and even an airplane fighter pilot had been killed as a consequence of his high-altitude pursuit of the UFO. The radar evidence and the unusual, contradictory aspects of the dynamics of the warplane crash site convinced Miller that this UFO may indeed have been under the control of intelligent beings from an extraterrestrial source, and the intriguing testimony of an eyewitness farmer who had watched the final descent of the aircraft strongly reinforced Miller's belief.

Having established a television-servicing business with a friend around 1952, they set up a "listening system" in 1954 that included a reel-type tape recorder. After a long period of patience, a message was received in which a voice said that Richard Miller, albeit unaware of it, was a good telepathic communicator for them, and many subsequent interchanges occurred between 1955 and 1979. To prove their true identity and their advanced (only to denizens of Earth) scientific knowledge, they instructed Miller and his group to be at a remote, secluded location in their state of Michigan at 2 a.m. Since the voice and message seemed so authentic, the group complied and was shockingly amazed when a domed, disk-like vehicle landed near them. Richard Miller was invited aboard to examine their spacecraft, and he (telepathically?) was told that the number 9(!) was the key to their vehicular construction and that the interstellar speed at which they journeyed did not have to exceed the "9th level" of their scale regarding transportational velocities.

During the course of about twenty-five years of astounding, enlightening information that the "space friends" had imparted to the group, a discourse regarding the Great Pyramid (not the alien's term for this huge structure) eventually was presented for their serious contemplation. They said that about 47,000 Earth years ago they had established an "outpost" and "beacon" for their purposes at the site where the Great Pyramid later was built, and in fact that the Pyramid was constructed over the *same* place where they had driven a shaft 243 (= 9) feet under the spot where the present so-called Subterranean Chamber is located. They said that powerful generators had been installed for two reasons, one being to "eliminate an alarming degree of axial excursion present at Earth's north and south poles." They revealed various dimensions of this structure, and *all* of the multiple-digit measurements could be reduced to the basic number 9! This is surprising enough, but their concluding remark was truly startling, and yet quite understandable to this author. Their leader said, "You will notice, my brothers, that all figures I have mentioned are multiples of the number 9, the reason being that 9 is the key to the mathematical science dealing with magnetics." Obviously, he was referring to the anti-gravitational mode of propulsion of their space vehicles and their structural work on three-dimensional planet Earth. Hence, it is no wonder that many UFO reports mention that the vehicles were soundless and appeared to possess a levitation capability, and even the Edgar Cayce spiritual source stated that the Great Pyramid had been built via anti-gravitational forces.

CHAPTER 5

The Mayan Sacred Calendar/Tzolkin Chronology and the Spiritual Evolution of Humankind

For many people in the world, the Mayan, Aztec and Incan cultures were extremely low-consciousness, especially regarding the apparently frequent practice of human sacrifice. So how could the Maya have created a complex timetable/ matrix concerning human spiritual evolution? Many dubious persons, especially in North America, view the Maya as ignorant aborigines, just as Spanish conquistador and adventurer, Hernan Cortes, did when he arrived in the New World in 1519. Therefore, a sufficient degree of credibility and probability demands to be established in this matter. The intricacies, complexity and chronology of the Mayan calendar/Tzolkin have induced one highly-educated researcher and calendar interpreter to conclude that the Mayan high priests, or the real calendar's creator, had come to planet Earth from an extraterrestrial source. However, a spiritually-oriented, detailed and objective study of the Mayan calendar by Swedish Dr. Carl Johan Calleman has led him to conclude that the Tzolkin is a precise instrument that depicts the predestined spiritual evolution of humankind via the application of the number 9 (nine spiritual Creation Cycles), which is this author's numerical designation for the *destiny* of humankind.

Perhaps the Edgar Cayce spiritual source of ancient historical information can provide a satisfactory solution to this mystery and dilemma, beginning with Reading 364-4 that pertains specifically to the so-called lost continent of Atlantis, which, quite literally, was located in a large area of where the Atlantic Ocean now sits directly above the sunken continent, which the Cayce tested source offered much detailed information about pertaining to its long history and final, self-induced destruction. Moreover, the geological knowledge of massive plate tectonics adds credence to the Cayce story. The Cayce spiritual information also revealed that the Christ Soul had entered physical embodiment as Amelius, who became the original ruler at the beginning of Atlantis and where the *red* race of humankind was installed by God/Creative Forces. (Incidentally, what is now the east coast of America had been the lowlands of Atlantis, and the people that the Pilgrims called the "red men" were the Atlantean descendants, according to the Cayce source.) The Christ Soul, as Amelius (think *ameliorate*, which means to improve or make better), created special calendars and charts regarding "signs, seasons, days and years" that most likely pertained to cosmology, chronology, astrology and numerology.

Much later, during the catastrophic breakup and submergence of Atlantis that the Cayce source said was manifested by and connected with the greedy, selfish, materialistic lifestyle of the Atlantean inhabitants, many refugees fled to the Yucatan area that is now a part of Mexico. The Cayce source, while still reading the Akashic Record or Book of Life, continued its perusal of the Record by saying that these refugees "...carried with them all those forms of Amelius that he gained through that as for signs, for seasons, for days, for years. Hence, we find in those various portions of the world, *even in the present day,* [author's emphasis] some form of that as was presented....." The Cayce reading ended by revealing, surprisingly, that Amelius (Christ Soul) later returned to the earth plane as Adam, the progenitor/father of our present Adamic race. This readily explains why Jesus/Jeshua referred to Himself as the "Son of man!" (Incidentally, the Cayce stenographer had misspelled the name Amelius as "Amilius", and she noted this probability at the end of Reading 364-4, since she had never heard this name in all the prior Cayce readings. However, much later the psychic readings via trance medium Ray Stanford of the Association for the Understanding of Man applied the correct name of Amelius, and further stated that our present word, *ameliorate,* as stated above, means to make better or more tolerable. This word originally was derived from the Atlantean name of the Christ Soul, and it has a very interesting etymology. Albeit originating in 1542 as the word, *meliorate*, in 1767, it was mysteriously changed to the present *ameliorate*. But strangely in 1877, the word, *meliorism*, appeared that pertained to the belief that the world tends to become better and that humans can aid its betterment, albeit present conditions strongly contradict this philosophy. This improvement concerning all souls in human physical embodiment was the initial mission of the Christ Soul as Amelius in Atlantis, and later would enter a series of earthly incarnations that would culminate as Jesus/Jeshua of Nazareth, according to the Edgar Cayce spiritual source of information.)

Many books have been written about the Mayan Sacred Calendar/Tzolkin and the cultures of the Mayan and Aztec peoples, but not so much about the Incan culture, albeit the Cayce source indicated that many of these three groups originated from the Atlantean refugee exodus, which really occurred more than once. The Cayce source even referred to the land of "Og/Inca" where the first migration of Atlantean refugees had fled to, obviously trying to get as far away as possible from the series of cataclysms that were destroying their homeland. However, the Cayce source also mentioned that some of the inhabitants of Lemuria/Mu came as refugees to Central America when their vast continent also slid beneath the waves that now comprise the Pacific (peaceful?) Ocean. Perhaps this is when the Andes Mountains were formed and even high-altitude places like Machu Picchu in antediluvian times had been merely a little higher than sea level. So it would appear that miscegenation has been a considerable factor concerning the peoples of Central and South America, and history tells us that Hernan Cortes also played a strong part in this genetic amalgamation process.

Most of the Mayan calendar books focus on the prophecies and chronology that are predicted and calculated to end at the winter solstice of December 21, 2012, and the scenario sometimes involves the manifestation of *fear* because it is associated with the unknown, much like the Book of Revelation in the Holy Bible. Even television programs have been proliferating, and presently are increasing in intensity, that are focusing on the "doomsday" aspect of the Mayan calendar prophecy, and this is exacerbated by the misinterpretation of many of the Nostradamus quatrains, which really can be applied to many conditions that have manifested since the publication of his book. Alternatively, Dr. Carl Johan Calleman's very spiritually-oriented book, The Mayan Calendar and the Transformation of Consciousness, concentrates on the nine (9) Creation Cycles (spiritual evolutionary periods concerning all of humankind) and also on their associated 9-step pyramids in the Yucatan Peninsula area of Mexico. Even Dr. James J. Hurtak's spiritual science book, The Book of Knowledge: The Keys of Enoch, mentions the importance of these pyramids in Central America, especially the group that forms a "tetrahedral pattern", with the pyramid at Palenque serving as the apex of this tetrahedral configuration. His book even describes a group of nine (9) pyramids that "interlock to form a Star of David." (see Key 1-0-5 of the book)

Another important deviation from the contents of other Mayan calendar books is Dr. Calleman's ending date for the nine (9) Creation Cycles that signify the spiritual evolution of humankind (each Cycle is a time period that is twenty times shorter that the preceding one, so the last one in 2011 is very short, comparatively). Whereas humankind is nearing the end of the present extremely materialistic eighth (8 is the strongest material number in the spiritual science of numerology) Galactic Cycle that will be completed in February of 2011, the final very spiritual Universal Cycle will cover about a 9-month period from early February to October 28, 2011 (not 2012), which is, ironically, the same time period for the gestation period that is required to create a *normal* human being. This last Cycle involves the brief time period when humankind is supposed to be in complete harmony and Love while experiencing Enlightenment. Of course, such a state of bliss seems utterly impossible at this time of extreme materialism, but, as suggested previously, perhaps a renegade asteroid, comet or other frightening cosmic scenario will engender the necessary anxiety and fear to coerce people to plead for help from their Creator or at least some form of higher power. As the anonymous battlefield philosopher claimed, "There are no atheists in foxholes!" Of course, there always is the possibility of public contact with benevolent extraterrestrials. Perhaps the Christ Spirit will permeate the hearts and minds of all human beings–or even appear physically again!

The extended calculated ending date of December 21, 2012, that many people in the world are now fixated on pertains to the so-called Mayan Long Count, which, according to Dr. Calleman, is correct regarding the archeological aspect of the Mayan calendar. However, the year of 2012 must be a highly unusual period concerning some type of human transformation to a different state of physical being that should be based on the successful completion of the final Universal Cycle in 2011. The Edgar Cayce spiritual source and the spiritual source that provided the awesome, spiritual science information that is contained in Dr. Hurtak's provocative masterwork, The Book of Knowledge: The Keys of Enoch, have mentioned a new "fifth root race" that will be created via a transitional phase from the present three-dimensional physical vehicle of expression for each soul. Perhaps the year 2012 will be the crucial, culminating period concerning some form of human cellular metamorphosis that will result when the human physical form transcends the fourth dimension of *time* and enters a fifth dimension to become a "Whole Light Being" as described in Dr. Hurtak's book. This may appear to be utterly ridiculous, but Christ said that *all* things are possible with God!

Before discussing the most pertinent numbers and time periods of the Mayan Sacred Calendar, we need to establish the true identity and mission of the mysterious entity who was known as Quetzalcoatl (Aztec) and his direct counterparts, Kukulcan (Maya) and Viracocha (Inca). Collectively, these three spiritual deities were known and addressed as "Thunapah" throughout the vast area of Central and South America.

Just as the tested, validated and valuable Edgar Cayce enlightening spiritual information indicated that the true identity of the architect of the Great Pyramid in Egypt had been Hermes (Christ Soul incarnation) and that the most likely source of the Mayan Sacred Calendar (Tzolkin matrix) was Amelius (the Christ Soul in Atlantis), the Ray Stanford (Association for the Understanding of Man) psychically-derived information revealed that Quetzalcoatl, Kukulcan and Viracocha (all called Thunapah) were one and the same entity: the Christ disciple, Didymos Thomas, who was also referred to as the "White God in the Americas" by the Ray Stanford spiritual source of information. In this case and discussion, a member of the White (purity) Brotherhood of Ascended Masters, Kuthumi Lahl Singh, who humbly preferred to refer to himself merely as "K-H", offered a lengthy, detailed discourse on this "White God in the Americas." (Incidentally, another member of this Brotherhood previously had divulged that Kuthumi had been the renowned Greek philosopher, Pythagoras, in a previous incarnation.) Kuthumi ("K-H") explained that Thomas, after receiving and assimilating the gifts of the Holy Spirit at Pentecost, was sent to India (Asia) for his assigned mission, and later to South and Central America. [Incidentally, there is a large monument to this Christ disciple, Didymos Thomas, at Chennai (formerly Madras) in southern India, where he was martyred after his return from the Americas because he had converted a king's family to Christianity.]

82

Having arrived first in Viru (now Peru) in his later years of life, Didymos Thomas began to teach the Christ philosophy everywhere along the coastal areas and also far inland, extending northward to Mexico and Central America, wherever the Holy Spirit guided and directed him to go, and this certainly may have involved a metaphysical teleportation process concerning the vast area that Thomas had to cover for his teachings. Like the Master Jesus, his Jeshua, Thomas talked to all these peoples in parables and perplexing symbolism. However, in their ignorance (just as still exists in the present) some of his teachings were misinterpreted and misunderstood. When he spoke of offering their hearts to God and Christ, the Son of God, this later translated into actually removing the hearts of their own selected martyrs and also the hearts of their captive enemies, which obviously was more desirable regarding normal self-preservation and for relieving social pressures. They would offer these excised gift hearts to the Sun (of) God, assuming that they were pleasing the Son of God, Jesus the Christ, that Thomas had convinced them of as being their Saviour. His presumed description of circumcision, which was so important to Jews since the practice had been directed by God to Abraham (obviously concerning hygiene), later morphed into the less-severe, common act of blood-letting from merely a pierced penile foreskin, as now can be understood by viewing the wall drawings that have been discovered in Central America. When Thomas mentioned a lion during his teachings, they had to substitute a jaguar because a lion was unknown to them in South and Central America. The jaguar ceremonial headdress was thus created by the natives.

Regarding the ship that Thomas had arrived in from Asia and from which he taught all along the coast, the natives were very impressed with the imposing, serpent-like bowsprit of the ship and soon began to refer to him as the "plumed serpent" (a term that involved the headdress that he wore later), and also because they assumed he had come from the "land of the serpent." His popularity became widespread and many gifts were bestowed upon him, especially the assembled feathers from the beautiful, colorful quetzal, their prized bird, and thus the name Quetzalcoatl was born. To please the people who admired him so much, Thomas wore these feathers in the form of a headdress, which, as stated, initiated the term "plumed serpent."

Thomas also told them that Christ had been known also as the "bright morning star", which induced them to begin worshiping the planet, Venus (the bright morning and evening "star"), which they also applied to Thomas himself because he often had spoken of his *own* oneness with God, especially whenever he became overwhelmed with the power of the Holy Spirit. Eventually, Thomas was even identified as the *spirit* of Venus, and then this planet became an integral component of their religion, primarily because this Jesus/Jeshua had never been presented to them in physical form.

In his deeply-intuitive, spiritually-inspired interpretation of the Mayan Sacred Calendar, as depicted in his informative, detailed, provocative book, The Mayan Calendar and the Transformation of Consciousness, Dr. Calleman refers to Kukulcan/Quetzalcoatl as the "carrier of the energy 9lk"— always the 9—and further calls this the "same energy as that of the Christ." He also states that Venus was seen as a manifestation of Quetzalcoatl and Kukulcan. This obviously validates and reinforces the Kuthumi elucidation and description of all of these mysterious aboriginal deities and spiritual teachers as having been the one person/entity, Didymos Thomas. Dr. Calleman even dedicated his book to Quetzalcoatl, referring to him as the "heavenly Creator of the Sacred Calendar" and the Maya as the "carriers of its truth." Assuming that the original calendar (Tzolkin matrix) had been a creation of the Christ Soul as Amelius, perhaps Didymos Thomas was responsible for the updating of this spiritual evolutionary timetable to apply to the last 5,000 years of the spiritual evolutionary process of humankind as the Adamic race. Of course, it is more likely that the Christ Spirit was the Mastermind of the entire philosophy and evolutionary scenario, just as the Christ Spirit manifested the surrealistic vision that John witnessed and later recorded to be presented in the New Testament as the fantastical, phantasmagorical Book of Revelation.

As a further validation of the true identity of Quetzalcoatl/ Kukulcan/Viracocha (Thunapah) as the Christ disciple, Didymos Thomas, the Calleman Matrix prophecy chart shows the time periods of rule by the thirteen (13 is a potent spiritual number) deities of the Mayan religion. The calculated time period for the rule of Quetzalcoatl is shown as 40-434 C.E. (a spiritually-tragic change from A.D., which seems to be at least a subliminal way of denying or even mocking Christ during these "last days" of the Piscean Age). This covers the time period when Thomas would have taught the Christ philosophy and mission. Dr. Calleman's created chart even refers to Quetzalcoatl as the "god of light" (Christ description) during this Heaven 9(!) period of the total thirteen (13 again) Heavens.

Since there are less than three years (2008–2010) left of the extremely "terracentric" (term from a channeled spiritual source that was describing humankind's current fixation on materialism) 8th Galactic Creation Cycle of the Mayan calendar countdown, perhaps a more detailed and comprehensive analysis is required for obtaining a better understanding of this crucial period. The inclusion of the prime spiritual sciences of numerology and astrology should provide more clarification, especially since 2008 is a number 1 (2+0+0+8 = 10 = 1) world year of new beginnings for all of humankind. With the three *consciousness* and *transformation* planets, Uranus, Neptune and Pluto transiting the zodiacal signs of Pisces, Aquarius and

Capricorn, respectively, they collectively are indicating that humankind is experiencing a "purification phase" that Christ described as the "birth pangs of the New Age" (transition from Pisces into Aquarius) in Matthew 24. Pisces is the sign of *suffering* and Aquarius is the New Age sign. Uranus activating Pisces denotes revolution and change via suffering, selflessness and humanitarianism—indeed, even to the point of martyrdom. Neptune is the spiritual planet in the revolutionary and humanitarian—albeit a detached humanitarianism—sign of Aquarius and the New Age, and this will continue until the critical year of 2012 that is viewed with foreboding by so many unenlightened people in the world today. Lastly, Pluto, as stated previously, represents consciousness (per Cayce spiritual source) and transformation (per astrology), as well as the death and rebirth (and hence also sex) of the associated 8th solar house for Pluto. Moreover, Pluto just entered the extremely material sign of Capricorn in January, 2008, and following a brief retracement in Sagittarius (religion, philosophy, higher education, law and long-distance travel) until late November, will resume its long transit of Capricorn until about 2024. Hence, the material world and the domain of big business and governmental leaders and all hierarchies (including the Vatican) will be drastically affected and even violently altered or eliminated by the demoralized, angry masses. The materialistic effect of Pluto in Capricorn will be intensified in 2008, especially after August, because gigantic Jupiter (expansiveness and excessiveness) in also transiting Capricorn for all of 2008. The entire outer-planet scenario can be viewed as a "spiritual conspiracy", especially when the planetary *aspects* are included and combined with the above collective scenario. Hence, it should become increasingly more difficult to transcend this intensely materialistic 8th Galactic Creation Cycle to qualify for participation in the experience that is designated for the ninth (9) and last Universal Creation Cycle of 2011 concerning Love and Enlightenment.

Again regarding the predicted fifth-dimensional "Whole Light Beings" that will comprise the new "fifth root race" (perhaps in 2012), Dr. Hurtak`s seemingly omniscient source of spiritual information and the realm of spiritual science described this fifth dimension as "the next *garment of light* that our matter-energy body enters in the process of spiritual evolution, a less-gross, material body with the restored *similitude* of God governing the physical processes." Dr. Hurtak continued by saying that his spiritual source explained that three-dimensional humanity will be transposed into the fifth dimension (obviously a Light realm) upon completing their education in this realm of "image and similitude." Simply expressed, it appears to be all about a synthesis of faith, hope and love, as the apostle Paul taught to all the Gentiles.

To further support Dr. Calleman's calculated ending date of October 28, 2011, as the last day for the time period of all nine (9) Creation Cycles, the Sun (capitalization for astrology) will be strongly influencing the zodiacal sign of Scorpio, which pertains to *death* and *rebirth*, indicating that the very limited, three-dimensional Homo sapiens will be reborn or reconstituted into a Light body because the solar 8th house of Scorpio also pertains to *regeneration*. To augment the scenario for the last day (October 28) of the Universal Creation Cycle, dynamic Jupiter (representing Father/Mother God) will offer a boost of positive energy as it trines the zodiacal sign of Taurus (first of the three earth signs, which, in this case, could pertain to the final *physical* form of human beings).

Another seemingly significant factor that might have a dynamic effect on the anticipated spiritual events of the final Mayan Sacred Calendar year of 2012 could be generated by the scheduled return of the aurora borealis (northern lights) and aurora australis (southern lights). Being electrical and electromagnetic in nature, perhaps the Master Cosmic Plan has included this amazing phenomenon and *light* show to interact with the photonic component involved with the bodily metamorphosis of human beings. Like the simple firefly/ lightning bug, this transition to a "whole light being" may also involve an electrochemical process acting on each cell of the human body. As a final commentary, other cosmic energies may be involved in the whole 2012 scenario because Dr. Hurtak also was told by his spiritual source that our entire solar system— and even our entire Milky Way Galaxy!—will pass through an "electromagnetic null zone" that will serve as a component of the human evolutionary process and destiny.

Since the planet Venus held such prominence in the religion and philosophy of the Maya (most likely because of its personification as the Christ disciple, Didymos Thomas/ Kukulcan/Quetzalcoatl), the paired, eight-year-interval Venus solar eclipses ("transits") apparently had a tremendous effect on the Mayan people and their high priests, who obviously understood the full meaning and details of their Tzolkin that present researchers and interpreters call the Mayan Sacred Calendar, especially as it would have been taught by their deity, Kukulcan (Thomas). The chronology involved with the planet, Venus, reveals that five synodical cycles of 583.92 (= 27/9) days comprise about eight years. Venus phases were seen as symbolic of the process of death and rebirth and these were linked to Quetzalcoatl/Kukulcan (Thomas), who must have revealed the truth about human reincarnation to them, just as Jesus/Jeshua had done with his disciples, especially concerning Himself (Melchizadek) and John the Baptist (Elijah). The latest Venus eclipse of the sun occurred on June 8, 2004, right in the midst of the present very materialistic Galactic Creation Cycle. Its counterpart or twin eclipse will occur on June 6, 2012 (!), which should have a greater spiritual implication because all of this date's numerals (6-6-2-0-1-2) total and vibrate to the number 17 of *suffering* and *redemption.*

However, just as Noah's great ark had grounded mercifully on the 17th day of a month, this second Venus eclipse of the sun (Son) should signify a *final* redemption for humankind, or rather for only those who have passed the test and experience of the ninth (9) and last Universal Creation Cycle that is the 9-month period in 2011. The so-called "rapture" that is depicted in Matthew 24 likely will be a powerful factor in this finalizing spiritual evolutionary scenario.

Concerning the possible effect(s) on the human brain, Dr. Calleman's comprehensive, detailed historical research regarding prior paired Venus solar eclipses (transits), especially the previous pair of eclipses (1874 and 1882), revealed that the development of Earth to a "Global Brain" began with the founding of the World Post Union news media and the laying of the telegraph cable across the Atlantic Ocean. Additionally, the telephone was invented by Alexander Graham Bell during the same double-Venus eclipse 8-year cycle. During the present Venus paired-eclipse cycle (2004 and 2012), the World Wide Web of the global computer Internet system certainly has greatly expanded the "Global Brain", perhaps to the extent of becoming overwhelmed with valid and invalid information, indicating that everything is polarized. Dr. Calleman wrote that the development of this Global Brain has been favored by the energies of the "katuns", which are periods of 20 x 360 (a biblical year was comprised of 360 days that vibrated to the number 9) days that equal 7200 days or 19.7 years of the Mayan calendar chronology in which the Venus eclipses (transits) have occurred. It definitely should be noted and realized that 7200 = 9 (the critical human *destiny* number) and 19.7 = 17 (that fateful number vibration again). Dr. Calleman feels that these celestial events somehow have served to concentrate these energies and have sent an "intensifying beam" of energy to planet Earth, and this author feels that this concept may be connected with the cosmic radiating energies and forces referred to in the Fatima Prophecy (see Chapter 7) and Dr. Hurtak's complex spiritual-science book, The Book of Knowledge: The Keys of Enoch.

Regarding the nine-(9)step pyramids in Central America that (according to the Edgar Cayce spiritual source) were built by the Atlantean refugees (now called the Maya?) and later some other people (probably Lemurian/Mu refugees), the Pyramid of the Jaguar in Tikal is 144 (9) feet high, and this measurement probably is connected with the 144,000 (another multiple of the human destiny number 9) days of a Baktun period of the Mayan Sacred Calendar. It seems much more than merely a coincidence that this large number is also the total number of members of all twelve tribes of Israel. Moreover, there are 144,000 Ascended Masters in the hierarchy of God/Creative Forces, and this number is specifically cited in the very culminating Book of Revelation in the Holy Bible.

Concerning the holy number 108 (9) of the Mayan calendar/Tzolkin that in the East (Asia) symbolizes wholeness and completeness (Buddhist priests strike their huge gongs 108 times), the nine (9) Creation Cycles of the calendar have twelve (12 is the number of perfect structure) transformations between Heavens (9 x 12 = 108), which is the total number of transformations between heavenly energies in the Mayan calendar system. Since the number 9 pertains to the destiny of humankind and the number 12 is the basis of measurement for all perfect structures, it becomes evident why the number 108, being the product of 9 x 12, is so very important in the spiritual evolutionary process of humankind.

Concerning a correlation of the Mayan Sacred Calendar with the human anatomy, Dr. Calleman notes that there are 13 (Christ with the 12 disciples) major joints in the human body, with 7 above and 6 below the waistline (umbilical) that correspond to the 7-Day and 6-Night periods of each Creation Cycle. Humans have 20 fingers and toes, and 13 x 20 = 260 days/units of the calendar. There are 20 different primary amino acids and 260 different distinct cell types in the human body. Of course, the Tzolkin matrix or Sacred Calendar, which is also referred to as the Harmonic Module, has 260 (13 x 20 rows of squares or boxes) units that each contain dots and bars for counting, whereas the English alphabet has eliminated the cipher (0) to minimize it to present a more manageable and functional 26 letters, albeit this seems to be incomplete because one more letter (perhaps a vertically-reversed "Y") would accommodate the much more ideal number 27! Obviously, the number 26, which seems to pertain to the whole concept of spiritual evolution, is indicating the present status of humankind's incompleteness as perfected souls, just as the hypotenuse (soul/spirit) of the Pythagorean Divine Triangle (Life Theorem) indicates when it is *wholistically* interpreted (see next chapter).

Concerning the 7 endocrine glands of the human body that are associated with the 7 primary energy centers/vortices called chakras, Dr. Calleman suggests that an 8th chakra may be manifesting during this very materialistic 8th Galactic Creation Cycle that will end in early February of 2011. This implies that a 9th (!) chakra may be manifested during the 9th and last Universal Creation Cycle in 2011. To augment and substantiate this hypothesis, Dr. Hurtak's revelatory spiritual information reveals that these 8th and 9th chakras/energy centers *already* exit, but these two chakras appear to be located externally, obviously above the head, and yet within the electromagnetic/electrostatic auric field of the human body. At present, electromagnetic photography can detect and visually portray in real time the activity of the *internal* chakras/energy centers, but it would appear that a search for and investigation of the external chakras is warranted. However, these last two chakras may be too subtle and inactive at this current phase or stage of humankind's spiritual evolution.

Having mentioned the energy centers/chakras of the human body and its postulated possible transition to a fifth-dimensional "Light Body", Dr. Calleman has suggested the probability of "the healing of many diseases that may become much easier as the filters that are blocking the divine light disappear" during the present three-year (2008–2010) ending phase of the Galactic Creation Cycle. Astrology supports this probability because Saturn (duty, discipline, rewards and cause-and-effect) recently (September, 2007) began its transit (to 2010) and activation of Virgo, which is the zodiacal sign that is associated with the solar 6th house of work and *health*! This two and one-half-year astrological influence should assure that a serious attempt will be made by many people and governments to provide their suffering fellow human beings with adequate health care and/or medical insurance. However, for at least Americans, this massive medical aid will necessitate the printing of billions of more fiat money by a government/nation that already is truly bankrupt when the facts are confronted undauntingly. Of course, this scenario *could* be avoided if the promise of Saturn materializes via the discovery of genuine healing agents—even panaceas for such pandemics as AIDS—by some dedicated, intuitive medical researchers, and it seems that XENON may provide the basis for the actualization of this idealistic scenario. Indeed, since 1987, this author has proclaimed, even unequivocally, that the common blueberry (genus *Vaccinium*— vaccine?), with its ellagic acid and other special constituents and antioxidants, is ideal for *rejuvenating* the human body. However, since most willful people will not change their nutritional habits and lifestyle, their bodies may have to be rejuvenated again and again, unless there is a *regenerative* cellular process. Hence, the noblest of the noble gases can come to the rescue and *regenerate* the human body, especially from the effects of its natural blue light that research has proved is ideal for phototherapy. Alas, this is all too simplistic for the professional medical industry—it certainly is an *industry* now! (Incidentally, in 1943, the Edgar

Cayce spiritual source, while psychically prescribing blueberries as a remedy for a woman with multiple sclerosis and *general anemia*, parenthetically stated that blueberries contained a special property that "someone, someday, will use in its proper place." The world now seems to know of that proper place, according to the proliferation of blueberry-based articles in all of the printed news media.)

Since the medical importance and usefulness of xenon technology is being discussed and this book is primarily concerned with numbers, perhaps the numbers can serve as a catalyst for validating the veracity, or at least verisimilitude, of this author's supposition and hypothesis concerning xenon. On the scientific Table of Periodic Properties of the Elements, the noble gases are listed in Group 18 (the *time* number with its basic number 9 vibrational energy). Xenon has been assigned atomic number 54 (9) because it has 54 (9) protons and electrons in each of its atoms, which is quite unusual for a gas, thereby indicating its unique status as a chemical element and also the possibilities for special applications for humankind, perhaps even to act as a catalyst for raising consciousness by activating or increasing the "Ze'on thought particles" of the brain while a person meditates in the proximity of a xenon-filled plasma globe. Xenon vibrates to the potent ending number 27 because its letters, when converted to numerals, become 6-5-5-6-5 (= 27, the *triplication* of the number 9). Unfortunately for humankind, the air that each human breathes contains only about .09 parts of xenon in a million parts of air (ppm). (Incidentally, the same extraterrestrial source that divulged the number 9 measurement information that is presented in the last paragraph of the preceding chapter on the Great Pyramid also claimed that if a little more *xenon* existed in Earth's atmosphere humans would not be so inharmonious, aggressive and belligerent, especially regarding the killing of each other.)

Since the primary concern and topic of this book is the paramount number 9, the discussion and elucidation of the nine (9) spiritual evolutionary Creation Cycles of the Mayan Sacred Calendar should be sufficient to verify and validate the crucial importance of the number 9 concerning the destiny of humankind. However, the prevalence of the number 9 regarding *all* aspects of the Mayan calendar and its spiritual message indicates the pervasiveness and omnipresence of the number 9, as Dr. Jose`Arguelles depicts in his detailed, provocative, convincing treatise, The Mayan Factor: Path Beyond Technology. In his chapter called "The Numbers of Destiny", he wrote that 9 "is the key number related to computations that correlate to what we call time", which justifies its purpose as the *cyclic* number in the activities of humankind. In this same chapter, Dr. Arguelles cites a very significant phase regarding Mayan harmonics wherein the "avataric incarnation" of Pacal Votal (a great spiritual teacher) occurred. His existing "tomb" is very similar to the "coffer/sarcophagus" that is in the so-called King's Chamber of the Great Pyramid in Egypt. This "tomb" is dated A.D. 683 (= 17, the basic theme number in the Great Pyramid) and its entire structure at the Tower of the Winds at Palenque is very similar to the entire structure of the King's Chamber. As a reminder, the architect of the Great Pyramid was Thoth Hermes Trismegistus, an incarnation of the Christ Soul. The supreme importance of this deity, Pacal Votal, to the Maya is supported by the location of his "tomb" in the 9-story/step Temple of the Inscriptions, which is a pyramidal structure at Palenque where there also are sculpted representations of the Nine (9) Lords of Time. When again considering the number 17, perhaps it also may be significant, and not merely coincidental, that Pacal Votal's "tomb" was not discovered until 1952 (= 17). The extraterrestrial connection with the Maya, and specifically Pacal Votal, has been reinforced by the sculpture on the lid of his "sarcophagus" that appears to show an *astronaut* in a space vehicle. Referred to as a "Galactic Master", Pacal Votal declared himself to be a *serpent* (the Christ disciple, Didymos Thomas, as Quetzalcoatl, the "plumed serpent"?) and initiate and possessor of knowledge (what Thomas had received from the Holy Spirit at Pentecost). Perhaps this avatar, Pacal Votal, had been a later incarnation of Didymos Thomas/Quetzalcoatl because Dr. Calleman had referred to his (Quetzalcoatl) earthly incarnations as being "manifestations of the same energy as that of Christ." Once a spiritual seeker assimilates a thorough understanding of karma (law of cause-and-effect), then this supposition and hypothesis could become a truth, especially via an intuitive perusal of the Akashic Record or Book of Life.

Some other specific references and use of the number 9 in The Mayan Factor: Path Beyond Technology are cited in the following list:

1. The Nine Lords of Time and the Nine Lords of Night add to the number 18, which is two cycles of the number 9.
2. The *tun*, a 360-(9)unit "calendar" component of the Tzolkin, is called the *harmonic calibrator*.
3. The harmonic for each of Earth's magnetic poles is 144 (9).
4. The light harmonic of Earth is 288 (= 18/9). This number may have a correlation with the 288-foot diameter regarding the Aubrey Holes in the Aubrey Circle at Stonehenge, England.
5. In the sequence of fractal harmonics, the great Mayan number of synthesis is 13 66 560, whose collective 7 (spirit) numerals vibrate to the number 27 (*triplication* of the number 9).
6. The 9 steps or increments of the pyramids correspond to the 9 spiritual evolutionary Creation Cycles.

7. The departure of the "galactic masters" at the end of the ninth (9) Baktun (time period) corresponds spiritually with the cyclic number 9 of *endings*.

When many unenlightened people in the world look at the Tzolkin matrix, they naturally see only a rectangular chart of 260 squares that contain black and white dots and bars that easily can be interpreted to represent the numerals 1 through 5, respectively. So we justifiably may ask how only a few investigators and researchers can translate this matrix accurately to present the astounding, incredulous, prophetic information that is contained in such master works as The Mayan Factor: Path Beyond Technology and also The Mayan Calendar and the Transformation of Consciousness, the latter of which should be of great value to the dedicated spiritual seeker. Both of these researchers have presented a comprehensive elucidation that encompasses a grand spiritual philosophy, and their precise evaluations and interpretations indicate that a considerable amount of *intuition* must have inspired and accompanied their logic. The Edgar Cayce spiritual source mentioned a *superconscious* or *soul mind* that exists at a level below the conscious and subconscious areas of human consciousness. Since this soul mind has retained the memories of the soul's activities in previous incarnations/lifetimes, certain important dramatic and traumatic past-life experiences and episodes can migrate to the surface of the consciousness or psyche of an entity, especially during deep meditation and also during the subconscious dream realm. It follows that anyone who has an intense interest and focus on a particular subject or event, especially to the point of being an obsession, may have been involved strongly with it in one or more previous lifetimes, as the Cayce source indicated for various people during personal past-life psychic readings of the Akashic Record/Book of Life. This has been observed and documented for various children up to about the age of five years old because the physical brain is still in a formative stage, which permits these past-life memories to surface, especially the traumatic experiences of the entity, as Dr. Ian Stevenson's long, serious study indicated. Dr. Brian Weiss obtained the same results for adults via the application of regressive hypnosis.

The psychological condition that has just been discussed and evaluated may be applied to both Dr.Carl Johan Calleman and Dr. Jose` Arguelles, and both of these Mayan culture researchers may have been involved directly or indirectly with Quetzalcoatl (Christ disciple Didymos Thomas) and Pacal Votal (a possible and probable later incarnation of Didymos Thomas/ Quetzalcoatl). Since Dr. Jose` Arguelles is of Spanish descent and Central and South America are now populated with millions of Spanish descendants, his past-life connection to Mayan culture and history is quite probable. However, Dr. Calleman's intense focus on Mayan culture and history is an intriguing enigma because he was born and raised in Sweden, which definitely is not Mayan country, and this author's hypothesis was discussed with him in 2006 when his revealing, enlightening and valuable book was published. Dr. Calleman has a Ph.D. in *physical biology* and his avocation specialty is/was in *environmental health*. He took a "vacation" to Mexico at age 29, just when he was experiencing his first Saturn Return, astrologically, and Saturn is associated strongly with karma and *destiny,* both of which are based on past-life experiences. Since Saturn completes a full revolution of the sun every 29.5 years, its influence for every human being is especially strong between the ages of 29 and 30 when it has returned to the same position in a person's natal horoscope. This should be seriously considered regarding Jesus/Jeshua of Nazareth and why, after disappearing for 18 (time number) years, He returned to the Jerusalem area at "about age 30" (Luke 3:23 of The New English Bible and The Open Bible) to begin His predestined mission of presenting a New Covenant for and to humankind.

This author's personal experiences with both the first and second Saturn Returns resulted in surprising, unanticipated life changes. At age 30, I suddenly lost my industrial, white-collar, records keeping job and "serendipitously" was chosen to form a group of primarily ultrasonic test inspectors of nuclear fuel elements, albeit at that time I knew nothing about high-frequency sound as a probing medium for the internal inspection of industrial materials. The serendipity and synchronicity were involved when I applied for a job at a local industrial firm, and the plant manager—to my amazement—was the person that I had repaired three (!) television sets for only a short time before this meeting, and that was the first time I had met him in this lifetime. Apparently, he had been so pleased with my work on his TV sets that he said he wanted me for this type of work, which began a new 30-year avocation for me. The karmic aspect of this episode in my life was revealed 22 years later in 1982 when I received a soul-life psychic reading (see Introduction for this book) wherein it stated that when I had been "Ishmeola", an "engineer in Atlantis", I had worked successfully with the "sound disks" (ultrasound?) as they were applied for human cellular "decorporation methods." This further appears to explain why I am preoccupied with my intense belief that the human body can be *regenerated* via the utilization of high-frequency sound energy and the very noble gas, *xenon*, and its associated collective energy vibration of the number 27 augments and reinforces this factor.

During my *second* Saturn Return astrological influence at age 60, I had just completed the construction of a 20-foot-long ultrasonic automatic inspection system for my aerospace firm employer when "deteriorating conditions" compelled me to suddenly terminate this lucrative source of personal sustenance to become an "independent medical researcher" concerning the *xenon* technology as it could be applied for the cellular *regeneration* of the human body and extension of the present human life span, and also to raise human consciousness via activation/production of Ze'on thought particles.

[Incidentally, an in-depth understanding of the law of cause-and-effect (commonly called *karma*, and often facetiously) should induce and permit anyone to accept the truth that many persons of the black race today may have been *white* slave owners or traders in one or more previous lifetimes, or even merely an entity who strongly disliked the Negro race, and, therefore must experience the travails of the black race that still persist in global society and its varied sociological conditions. Of course, this racial reversal also applies to *all* of the five (number of man) races when negative karma is manifested and activated. The Edgar Cayce spiritual source explained this philosophy quite succinctly and ideally when it stated that all entities experience mandatory "sojourns" in the earth plane so as to "meet Self." Moreover, since "sex is the strongest force in man", according to the Cayce source and which is empirically obvious, this should assist anyone's understanding, tolerance and compassion concerning the recent proliferation of "sex changes" (transsexuals), especially from the male to female gender. This propensity regarding sexual identity usually is mentally formulated at a young age because the soul memories of when the person had enjoyed one or more lifetimes in a body of the opposite gender arise to the level of the conscious awareness, thereby inducing the person to manifest a strong desire to return to that experience(s). This occurs much more frequently with the male gender because the entity in *this* incarnation has been assigned—and accepted—a male body because it should offer the best prospects for successfully accomplishing the entity's mission in this lifetime. If the desire begins to manifest later in life, this could be induced when the male person has endured much hardship and suffering in his quest for material acquisitions and prominence, and thus engenders an intense feeling and desire to return to the former pleasant, passive female role of one or more previous lifetimes. Indeed, reincarnation and karma combine to offer a sensible explanation concerning *all* sexual orientations and identities, as well as any other human relationship factors and conditions. A notable example emanated from the psychic, spiritual source via Edgar Cayce in which it was stated that for most marriages the two people are really forced together to try to dissipate the severe negative karma that one or both of these two entities had perpetrated toward the other in one or more previous incarnations. Hence, marriage principally involves merely *desire* and romance, and may have very little to do with the true nature of *love*!].

CHAPTER 6

The *Wholistic* Meaning of the Pythagorean Divine Triangle (Life Theorem)

In Manly P. Hall's 1928 comprehensive, provocative and compelling treatise on metaphysics and the great mysteries of human life in the world, which he audaciously entitled, The Secret Teachings of All Ages, he referred to the great Greek teacher, Pythagoras, as the *first* philosopher, and his birth has been presumed to have occurred between 600 and 590 B.C. While his symbolic *tetractys* (an equilateral triangle that encloses ten evenly-spaced dots with tails, like human spermatozoa) may pertain to the number 10 destiny of the *soul* concerning ultimate human perfection, at this present stage and time of human spiritual evolution his Divine Triangle has a profound significance that is in complete accord and synthesis with the numbers and purpose of this book. Unfortunately, for most unenlightened people in the world, their knowledge and understanding of the Divine Triangle is limited to merely its mathematical nature and its associated Forty-Seventh Proposition of Pythagoras (erroneously attributed to Euclid, according to Manly Hall) that states that the sum of the square of the hypotenuse of a right triangle (90 degrees) is equal to the sum of the squares of the other two sides (see Figure 2).

Pythagoras said that the perpendicular side of the Triangle, with its assigned numerical value of 3, symbolically represents Mind, the base (4) represents Body, and the hypotenuse (5) represents Spirit/ Soul. His choice of the numbers 3, 4 and 5 obviously was not merely an arbitrary decision.

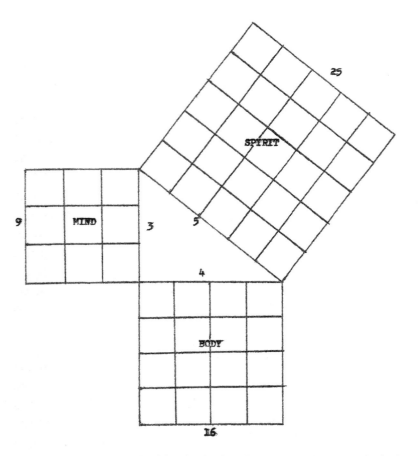

The numbers 3, 4 and 5 = 12, the basis of measurements in perfect structures, such as the new Jerusalem in the Book of Revelation in the Bible.

The numbers 9, 16 and 25 = 50, which is the Pythagorean Sacred Number and the vertical position of the King's Chamber at the 50th course of masonry/blocks in the Great Pyramid at Giza, Egypt.

FIGURE 2: The basic Pythagorean Divine Triangle (Life Theorem)

Since Pythagoras appeared to believe that all things consist of three (3) components, he, like Christ, emphasized the number 3 of the triangular nature of human beings and our three-dimensional reality. Of course, the Divine Triangle itself is comprised of three (3) sides, so it is an ideal configuration to symbolically depict the three basic human components of mind, body and spirit/soul. The number 4 of the base is also the number of sides to a square, like the base of the Great Pyramid in Egypt. The number 5 of the hypotenuse is also the *number* of man, and this number also assures that all three sides of the Divine Triangle combine to equal the number 12, like the 12 Christ disciples, and also is the measurement unit for creating a perfect structure, as revealed in the Book of Revelation regarding the *new* Jerusalem. The last of the five (5) Pythagorean geometric solids is the dodecahedron that has 12 pentagonal faces or components. Of course, the *sphere* already is perfect and obviously pertains to God or Creative Forces (an ideal Cayce source term).

When all three sides of the Divine Triangle are squared, the products of 9, 16 and 25 are obtained, and all three sums combine to produce the special number 50. This is called the Pythagorean Sacred Number that correlates with the vertical position of the King's Chamber at the fiftieth (50) course of masonry/blocks in the Great Pyramid, and also correlates with the specific, important 50-year period (1936–1986) that is designated by the time factor that begins with the King's Chamber, as calculated in Chapter 4. (Incidentally, this author was residing in a number 50 house in San Diego, California, when he was spiritually awakened to begin the long, arduous journey that has so far culminated with the composing of this book that, hopefully, will serve as a catalyst to propel a spiritually-inquisitive individual toward an investigation of metaphysics and the awesome Christ Philosophy.)

Considering the expanded, *wholistic* interpretation of the Pythagorean Divine Triangle (Life Theorem), the detailed elucidation was revealed via the same Association for the Understanding of Man's informational spiritual source that had divulged (via trance medium Ray Stanford) the astounding Quetzalcoatl/Didymos Thomas true identity regarding the Mayan Sacred Calendar/Tzolkin. Since this spiritual source (Kuthumi Lahl Singh, or "K-H", as he simply and humbly referred to himself) had been Pythagoras in an earlier incarnation (see Chapter 5), he chose to offer the members of A.U.M. a greater understanding of his Divine Triangle that would greatly transcend merely geometry and mathematics.

Instead of merely counting the small individual squares/ units of the three squared sides of the Triangle, Kuthumi (Pythagoras) said that we need to include the large encompassing square of each side of the Triangle so that 9 becomes 10, 16 becomes 17, and 25 now becomes 26 units. Hence, we now can see that the human destiny number 9 is expanded to include the soul destiny number 10. However, perhaps the most revealing factor of this wholistic version of the Triangle is that the base (Body) number 16 is now transformed into the number 17 of *suffering* and *redemption*, as was depicted in the monthly days (17) regarding the Great Flood-cleansing episode in Genesis. Basically, the base of the Triangle symbolically pertains to the physical and material aspects of earthly life, and Kuthumi here explained that the *physical* number 7 (as derived from the number 16), when combined with the *material* number 8 (as derived from the number 17) indicates that the soul only can be individualized and perfected by experiencing the vicissitudes and suffering of a sufficient number of physical incarnations in the earth plane of three-dimensional matter, but only after our karmic debts have been atoned for or dissipated sufficiently for qualification.

At this point in his explanation of the full meaning of the base of the Divine Triangle, Kuthumi interjected a surprising parenthetical remark that greatly expanded the meaning of the number 17 that also permeates the chapters of this book. To reinforce the material, physical and symbolical aspects of the base of the Triangle, Kuthumi revealed that the 17th (hydroxy) ketosteroid in the cortex of the human adrenal endocrine glands controls the factor of aging/ageing of human bodies, and this basically involves *stress*. The Edgar Cayce medical information also noted that the adrenals have a potent effect on all of the other six endocrine glands, obviously because so many hormones and chemicals are produced in both the cortex and medulla components of the two *triangular* adrenal glands.

Since Kuthumi's revelation seems to make perfect sense, medical science needs to redirect its urgent biophysical research concerning the aging/ageing process in the human body. In the meantime, we need to ingest as many antioxidants as possible, and this author's vivid dream in 1987 indicated that blueberries (as stated previously) provide a potent source of antioxidants, especially concerning the scourge of pandemic AIDS, and the scientist who assigned the genus, *Vaccinium*(!), to this berry species must have been aware of its health benefits, as global nutritional researchers are discovering. It should also be noted here that cranberries are classified in this same genus, and the juice of these red berries is effective for controlling urinary tract infections, but consuming a can of whole-berry cranberry sauce can eliminate even severe cases of UTIs, as this author has experienced.

Referring to Figure 3, we see that the basic 9 squares of side number 3 are encompassed by a large square, so now the 9 of Mind completes the process of Perfection (10). Since the number 10 reduces and vibrates to the number 1, Kuthumi said that this symbolizes the Holy Trinity as the 3-in-1 of

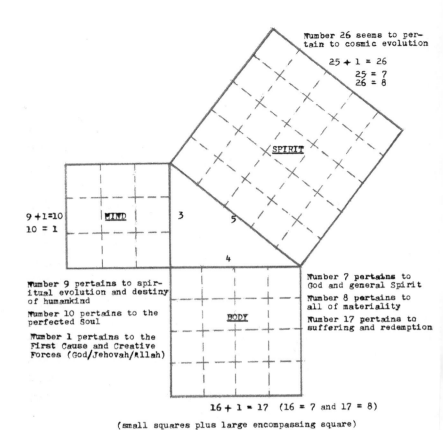

Number 26 seems to pertain to cosmic evolution

25 + 1 = 26
25 = 7
26 = 8

SPIRIT

9 + 1 = 10
10 = 1

MIND

3

5

4

Number 9 pertains to spiritual evolution and destiny of humankind

Number 10 pertains to the perfected Soul

Number 1 pertains to the First Cause and Creative Forces (God/Jehovah/Allah)

BODY

Number 7 pertains to God and general Spirit

Number 8 pertains to all of materiality

Number 17 pertains to suffering and redemption

16 + 1 = 17   (16 = 7 and 17 = 8)

(small squares plus large encompassing square)

FIGURE 3: Wholistic Pythagorean Divine Triangle

Father, Son and Holy Spirit. He also said that Mind (9) often procrastinates and is reluctant to progress to the full completion (10) of the required cycle for soul Perfection. Obviously, this would necessitate one or more further incarnations of the soul into human embodiment. With more than six billion (6,000,000,000) souls now in embodiment in the earth plane, it is evident that we have yet to become aware of our predestined real purpose of becoming LOVE individualized, as Jesus/Jeshua the Christ demonstrated for us via His ignominious crucifixion. [Incidentally, for those entities whose psyche functions solely at the logic level, the concept of reincarnation, when applied to six billion people in the world, appears to be unrealistic and even impossible. However, if they could accept the truth concerning the existence of the antediluvian continents of Atlantis and Lemuria/Mu and their large populations of the red and yellow races (as revealed in the Cayce spiritual information and other spiritual sources), then the concept of reincarnation and karma could become feasible. Indeed, a personal session of regressive hypnosis probably would reveal at least one traumatic experience that may have occurred to them while in physical embodiment on one or both of these continents.]

Referring again to the base or Body side (4) of the Divine Triangle, the number 8 that is obtained from the reduced wholistic number 17 also pertains to what Kuthumi described as the "8th supreme spiritual region" of at least our local universe and that extends beyond the seven (7) heavens that humans limit their consciousness to, especially regarding the seven (7) physical energy centers (chakras and endocrine glands). Kuthumi said that humans consider the seven spiritual centers, when projected to the archetypal level, as being seven spiritual planes. But, wholistically, there is an "8th plane" that may be understood through the physical body, and this even is relayed in the archetypal pattern of the human body. Therefore, this shows that the *physical* body is truly needed as a "spiritual temple." Obviously, we should ponder quite seriously the full magnitude of the damage we inflict upon this "spiritual temple" when we ingest prohibitive amounts of alcohol, tobacco, drugs, "junk food", etc. From a spiritual perspective, we actually are mocking God/Creative Forces when we willfully perform such acts that in reality are essentially a subconscious form of suicide that we euphemistically refer to as "being in denial." Apparently, even at the superconscious soul level, most humans are in denial regarding the spiritual evolutionary necessity of attuning our will (birthright) with the Master Will of the Creator/Father.

Continuing on to the hypotenuse (Soul/Spirit) and its basic number 5 side of the Triangle, the squaring of this side yields a total of 25 small squares, and this sum reduces to the primary spiritual number 7 that is mentioned many times in Genesis, and even fifty-two (52 again vibrates to 7) times in the Book of Revelation, as Dr. Carl Johan Calleman has observed. Ironically—but not really— this is the same number (7) that was derived from the *basic* squaring of the base (Body) of the Divine Triangle, thus indicating that the number 7 can refer to both the physical body as a temple for spirit and the spiritual soul itself, which again reveals that the soul *must* be "processed" through matter in order to be individualized and perfected.

As further evidence and emphasis of this spiritual philosophy, the *wholistic* number 26 for the hypotenuse reduces to the primary materistic number 8, which tends to integrate the Body and Spirit/Soul of sides 4 and 5 of the Divine Triangle. Additionally, the number 26 seems to be involved in the overall aspects of the human spiritual evolutionary process, especially as indicated in the 260 (26 with a cipher/multiplier) number units of the Mayan Sacred Calendar/Tzolkin, the 26 letters of the English alphabet, and even the approximately 26,000-year precessional cycle of the equinox that is also connected with the design, meaning and chronology of the Great Pyramid in Egypt.

Regarding a personal spiritual awareness and transformation for any person/entity, a unique and useful application of the *basic* squaring of the Pythagorean Divine Triangle, as the Life Theorem, has been illustrated by professional numerologists, Dusty Bunker and the late Faith Javane, in their very comprehensive book, Numerology and the Divine Triangle (1979). Utilizing the large, encompassing square for each of the three sides of the Triangle as a 27-year (triplication of the number 9) time marker/period, each of the three outside border lines represents a cyclic period of 9 years. As shown in Figure 4, the three squares pertain to three 27-year cycles of a person's life that also approximates the astrological Saturn Return cycles that are a primary integral component of an entity's natal horoscope. Rather than using the Pythagorean designations of Mind, Body and Spirit for the three squares of the Divine Triangle, the words Youth, Power and Wisdom are substituted, and these terms quite aptly designate the three main phases of a person's life in each incarnation.

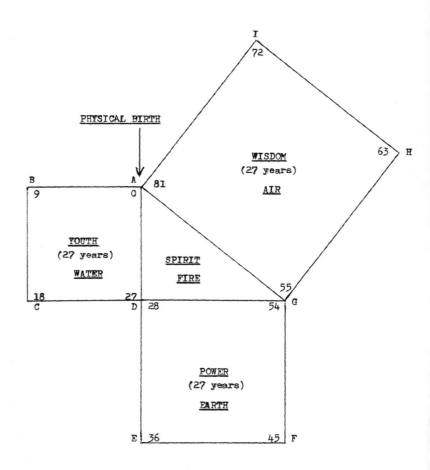

9- and 27-YEAR LIFE CYCLES of an ENTITY

(Place first 9 letters and their numerical values of first and middle
 names at spans A to I. If less than 9 letters, begin first name again)

FIGURE 4: Use of the Pythagorean Divine Triangle to
depict the activities of a human life span

110

When applying the Divine Triangle to function as a natal numeroscope for any particular individual, the first nine (9) letters of the alphabet are placed sequentially at the corners of all three squares. Then the sequential letters of the person's birth name (as it officially appears on the birth certificate) are placed at each 9-year side of all three squares, along with the numerical value of each of the letters of the birth name. It should be noted that only the first and middle (if there is one) names of the subject are used because the last or surname applies to the entire family, and therefore is not personal enough to provide an accurate delineation of the person's life pattern or "roadmap." If the first and middle names are too short in letters to accommodate the entire 81-year life span of the Triangle, then the first name is repeated to complete the nine (9) sides of all three squares.

The month, day and year of the birth date are placed at the three sides of the basic Triangle itself because the numerals of the birth date reveal the basic life lesson or purpose for the entity. The birth *name* indicates the second most important aspect of an entity's predestined life path/lesson because its letters, when converted to numbers, reveal the karmic lesson(s) that must be addressed, and hopefully dissipated, during the prospective lifetime. Hence, like it or not, numerology is really more important than astrology because the numbers basically apply to the *soul*, whereas astrological influences pertain mostly to the personality of the individual and all of the ramifications that this implies, and many people struggle all their lives with their personality, never discovering or realizing who they really are and why they have incarnated in a physical human body.

The Divine Triangle methodology may be too complicated for the neophyte in numerology, but it can reveal a more detailed scenario for an entity who is diligently seeking to learn as much as possible about his or her reason for being. The Holy Bible advises everyone to *know themselves*, and the Edgar

Cayce spiritual source was more forceful when it stated, "The great study of man should be Self. Study self; study self; study self!" Accompanying this instruction concerning a successful "sojourn" in any incarnation, the Cayce source further advised and urged that "patience, persistence and perseverance" should always be practiced.

CHAPTER 7

Significant Numbers of the Fatima Prophecy and Subsequent Spiritual Apparitions

The spiritual phenomena and events that occurred six (6) times at Fatima, Portugal, during a consecutive five- (5) month period (May 13 to October 13) in 1917, were preceded by three (3) angelic appearances in the spring, summer and fall of 1916. To analyze the meaning and significance of these numbers, quantities and dates, sequentially, the number 6 pertains to responsibility and adjustments, the number 5 is the number of man, change and the 5 races, and 13 is the powerful spiritual number (Christ with the 12 disciples) and, of course, May 13th is now commemorated by the Vatican and all Catholics as "Fatima Day." The year when this spiritual phenomena and dire message was fully presented was in 1917, which was when World War I was raging fiercely, and this was a time number 18 world year, numerologically (1+9+1+7). Moreover, the initial, specific date of May 13, 1917, contains 7 (prime spiritual number) numerals that collectively vibrate to the number 27 (5+1+3+1+9+1+7), which is a potent number of endings, being a triplication of the cyclic number 9.The number 3 is the *whole* number, especially since it pertains to the Holy Trinity of Father, Son and Holy Spirit and also applies to the 3-part and 3-phase nature of life in this 3-dimensional realm. The year of 1916 was a number 17 (1+9+1+6) world year of great suffering regarding World War I.

A well-versed, competent astrologer most likely could offer an augmenting assessment of certain negative, agitating and compounding planetary influences during 1917. Basically, Sun in Taurus (the *money* and *earth* sign—both pertaining to the *material* aspects of human life) at the beginning day of May 13 was wholly in accord with the contents of the Marian message which will be adequately discussed in this chapter.

After the third (3) Marian apparition on July 13, 1917 (the "Lady" appeared on the 13th of each month), at which approximately 5,000 people attended, the previously-selected (we can surmise) three (3) children later reported that they had been given a message that Lucia, who was the oldest at age 9 (!), had been instructed to later transcribe for release to the world in 1960 (a spiritual number 7 world year). The letter was passed on to the Catholic hierarchy at the Vatican, and all Catholics and denominations of Christians anxiously awaited the scheduled disclosure of its contents. However, the crucial year passed with no statement having been released from the Vatican. Then, seven (7) years later, a Vatican spokesman explained that Pope Paul VI had decided that the time was not appropriate to divulge the contents of the Fatima message of 1917, but the dire message and its prophecy will be revealed and evaluated later in this chapter, as stated above.

During the period from November 29, 1932, to January 3, 1933 (in the midst of a severe global economic depression), the same "Lady from Heaven" appeared at Beauraing, Belgium, a total of thirty-three times (the number 33 is called the "Christ Number" because of the 33-year messianic mission of the Christ Soul as Jesus/Jeshua, and also pertains to the highest 33rd degree of mastership in Freemasonry). Again, children were the recipients of the Marian apparitions, but these five (to reiterate, 5 is the number of man and the 5 races) children were older, ranging in age from 15 down to age 9. The obviously female apparition identified herself as the "Immaculate Virgin" that many thousands of people witnessed, especially during the last appearance on January 3, 1933, when Sun in Capricorn was influencing and activating the most materialistic interests of all humans.

Chronologically, the next recorded public Marian apparition occurred at Garabandal, Spain, during the evening of June 18, 1961 (18 is the time number that also vibrates to the basic destiny number 9, and 1961 was a number 1 world year of new beginnings, but more importantly, it was the year following the failed release of the Fatima message by the Vatican). Once again, children were the recipients of this initial spiritual Marian appearance and message that would be followed by many more appearances during the succeeding four (4 is a basic testing number) years. On October 18 (the time number again) of this same number 17 world year (1+9+6+1), the four (4) girls issued a public statement regarding a stern message that they had received from the "Lady" in which it demanded much "penance and sacrifice", which probably was engendered from the failed release of the Fatima message/letter.

As a parallel and continuing phase of the 1961 message, on an evening in June of 1962 (time number 18 world year) the girls viewed another Marian apparition and scenario that motivated and elicited terrifying screams from the girls that the witnessing crowd could hear. The horrific vision and chastisement was repeated the following night on the Feast of Corpus Christi.

Near the end of June in 1962, one of the girls was informed by the "Lady" that a "little miracle" would be performed for the girl on July 18 (again the time number) and that she should inform the public two weeks in advance. Late in the evening of the scheduled day, the girl stuck out her tongue for the crowd to clearly see, and then a host (Communion wafer representing the crucified body of Jesus/Jeshua) actually materialized on the surface of the girl's tongue.

The fourth anniversary of the Garabandal spiritual apparitions was on June 18, 1965, and this long series of Marian appearances would end on November 13, 1965. Again, we have the potent spiritual number 13, and the total of all the numbers of this date (1+1+1+3+1+9+6+5) vibrate to the number 27 of big endings.

With the obvious purpose of showing humankind that these continuing spiritual phenomena and messages were intended for all souls in embodiment in the earth plane, the next recorded event occurred at Zeitoun, a suburb of Cairo, Egypt. Evidently intended for maximal traumatic effect, especially concerning non-Christians, a series of glowing spectacles occurred above the Coptic Orthodox Church that theologians believe is the place in Egypt where Mary and Joseph, with the baby Jesus/Jeshua, had fled to (at an angel's direction) to avoid King Herod's massacre of all male children up to two years of age who resided in the Bethlehem area.

Beginning in April, 1968 (a number 6 world year of responsibility and adjustments), a Marian appartition appeared at the dome of the church, and this event proved to have been merely a harbinger for the *hundreds* of succeeding events that eventually would be witnessed by hundreds of thousands of people of various faiths and nationalities. Many photographs were produced to establish authenticity of the remarkable phenomena. The apparitional figures appeared to include Mary, Joseph and Jesus/Jeshua as both a baby and an older child (perhaps age 12 when He first began questioning, testing and teaching the Jewish religious leaders), and also hovering, gleaming white doves. The spectacular, active displays were so convincing that even some Muslims converted to Christianity! Many people with physical ailments reportedly were healed (perhaps some psychosomatically, just as Christ had promised and demonstrated when He said, "Your *faith* has made you whole"). The amazing apparitions continued for almost three years, perhaps symbolizing the full Christine Ministry, until early 1971 (again equals the time number 18). It is likely that the spiritual phenomena would have continued a while longer if the local government officials or personnel had not begun to sell tickets to the events, as reported.

Similar Marian apparitions later were reported to have occurred at the Serian Orthodox Church of Saint Peter and Saint Paul in Beirut, Lebanon.

Since all of the five cited spiritual phenomena occurred from 1916 (17) until the 1970s, perhaps further Marian apparitions became unnecessary, especially for Roman Catholics, when Polish Pope John Paul II (Karol Wojtyla) reigned from 1978 to 2005, when he returned to Spirit in his twenty-seventh (potent ending number 27) year of service, and having been the first non-Italian pope in 455 years. It seems ironic, and perhaps quite karmic, that he had entered embodiment in this incarnation with an assigned zodiacal sign of Taurus, which is the first *earth* sign that is associated with the solar 2nd house of money, and his books undoubtedly sold in the millions of copies. The spiritual lesson of Taurus is to learn the proper, ethical approach to obtaining money, and then to practice the proper, responsible way to utilize this acquired money, especially concerning benevolent behavior toward fellow human beings. To compound this Taurus scenario, his numerological number 8 life path/lesson appears to be a strong indication that he had had serious money and material issues in one or more previous incarnations, and his role as a prominent religious figure may have been predestined and intended for assisting with the atonement and dissipation of this karmic debt. Obviously, he must have used the huge amount of money generated from the sale of his books in a charitable way, assuming that he actually had been in receipt of such monetary compensation. Moreover, having been born on the eighteenth (18) day of May indicates that the reduced number 9 (1 + 8) humanitarian and compassionate vibration should have assisted in an increased degree of self-denial in material matters.

Concerning the secret message that the Vatican was required to divulge in 1960 (number 7 world year of spiritual matters), perhaps the papal prophecies of Irish holy man and doctor, Malachy, who lived from 1094 to 1148, can shed some light as to the probable contents of the Fatima secret letter. Since Malachy had proven to have been quite accurate regarding popes John XXIII (1958–1963), Paul VI (1963–1978), John Paul I (1978) and the late John Paul II (1978–2005), we should contemplate seriously the pontification of Pope Benedict XVI in connection with the Fatima prophecy. (Incidentally, please note that John Paul I reigned only 33 days, which may be associated with the Christ Number concerning the 33 years of the earthly life of Jesus/Jeshua, and all of these popes from 1958 to 2005 had chosen the very biblical, New Testament names of John and Paul. However, Benedict is a distinct deviation from this trend and perhaps a very important aberration to be duly considered.)

The canonized Saint Malachy predicted that the next to the last Catholic pope would be "of the glory of the Olive." The Benedictine Order is known as Olivtans, and they reportedly always believed that the successor to John Paul II would be associated with them, and Cardinal Joseph Ratzinger (a German!) chose the name Benedict XVI. His advanced age of 81 years (2008) shows that he is the oldest pope to be elected since 1730. Being philosophically quite different from his predecessor, he is a leading hardliner who even reportedly has stated that Anglicanism and Protestantism are "not proper churches", which is inflammatory, just as was his remark concerning Islam.

Saint Malachy predicted that Benedict XVI would be succeeded by a "final pope who would be like Satan, taking the form of a man called Peter, who will lead his flock amid many tribulations after which the seven-hilled city, Rome, the seat of the Vatican, will be destroyed and the dreadful Judge will judge the people." Perhaps this is one of the beguiling imposters that are mentioned in the prophecy of Jesus/Jeshua that is recorded in Matthew 24, a chapter that everyone in the world should read and study often in these apparent "last days" of the Piscean Age (2011 to 2012 per astrology, and astronomy and the Mayan prophecy seem to confirm this scenario).

Perhaps the following information may be the best source of the truth regarding the contents of the Fatima secret message/letter and why the Vatican has been so reluctant and even fearful to divulge its entire message to at least its Roman Catholic adherents. However, the reader should always engender an objective, intellectual and intuitive perspective and consciousness while perusing, processing and assimilating any information that has been proclaimed to be the ultimate Truth.

Like world-famous psychic trance medium Edgar Cayce, Ray Stanford, who was the founder of the Association for the Understanding of Man, was able to subordinate and alter his consciousness to a spiritual plane at which spiritual entities from the White (purity) Brotherhood of Ascended Masters could and would offer requested detailed information concerning any subject that was recorded in the Akashic Records/Book of Life, provided that the spiritual seeker(s) genuinely was pursuing illumination and enlightenment via the acquisition of true knowledge. Having pondered the possible contents of the Fatima message for many years, like millions of other people in the world, the members of A.U.M. asked the spiritual source if it might be reasonable for them to be apprised of the contents of the secret letter. Replying affirmatively, the source of the reading proceeded to give a group of discourses to the A.U.M. members between 1971 (world year that vibrates to the time number 18) and 1972 (number 1 year of new beginnings). Having also asked the spiritual source for the meanings and details regarding the four main Marian apparitions and phenomena, the resultant complete information was quite comprehensive and is compiled in the book, Fatima Prophecy (1972, A.U.M., Austin, Texas). These revelations from spirit are very convincing to many people because they appear to be authentic and to have a "spirit of truth", albeit appreciably incredulous.

Beginning with the Fatima, Portugal, Marian appearance and message of 1917 (18), the "Lady" had warned of the effect of the peoples of Asia turning to materialism, which now is blatantly obvious at this time (2008), especially in (capitalistic) Communist China and even normally spiritual India. The Mayan calendar prophecy, as interpreted by Dr. Carl Johan Calleman, appears now to be quite accurate regarding the "World Tree" and its reversal concerning the ideology, philosophy and economics pertaining to the world's two hemispheres, as well as for the two hemispheres of the human brain regarding intellect and intuition. As depicted in the Mayan calendar chapter of this book, the world is experiencing the final phase of the extremely materialistic 8th Galactic (Creation) Cycle that will end in early February of 2011. Combining the Christ prophecy in Matthew 24, the Mayan calendar prophecy, and also the unusual next four-year astrological scenario with its cross pattern (testing and suffering) of equinox and solstice points and their connection with Saturn, Uranus and Pluto, its seems very likely that humankind presently is experiencing its so-called "last days" that must occur prior to the promised and anticipated reappearance of the Christ Soul to guide us into a New Age of peace, harmony and LOVE. It should be realized that Jesus/Jeshua said that the great majority of people in the world would be completely oblivious to the critical time factor immediately preceding His return to the earth plane. The intense materialism and secularism that pervades humankind at the present time could be the prerequisite condition regarding the Master Soul's return.

The Spirit of the Mother of Jesus (as the source of the A.U.M. readings described the Marian apparitions) further quoted the Fatima message wherein it warned of the cause-and-effect karmic factor if the peoples of the world do not manifest and practice a spirit of peace. She said that the animosity and selfishness would result in the division of the world into two heavily-armed military camps (the U.S.A. versus China?). This tenuous, exacerbating situation eventually would focus on Israel (as it has) and later manifest into an unusual situation in which the United States of America and Russia (notice not the defunct Soviet Union regarding the *time* factor), along with some allies, would join forces in a war with the "yellow races", which obviously refers primarily to the behemoth, China. She said that others (Iran, and also Arab and Muslim countries?) would ally with these "yellow races" when this war would be triggered by events related to "the Arabians and what today are called the Israelis." It should be helpful that Vladimir Putin has been assigned a Libra basic personality that is always seeking for the "perfect" partner because this zodiacal sign is associated with the solar 7th house of Partnerships. Tragically, Russian President (at the time) Putin had hoped and expected that U.S. President George W. Bush would become that special partner, but the latter's willful and immoral war with Iraq subverted the formation of the arrangement. However, a President Barack Obama or Hillary Clinton should accommodate the predicted future American-Russian relationship.

To augment and corroborate this World War III scenario (3 is the whole number that indicates the strong possibility of a third world war), Dr. James J. Hurtak's spiritual source depicted a similar scenario that is described in The Book of Knowledge: The Keys of Enoch, wherein it states that a massive Chinese army will invade the "central lands of Russia" (perhaps the oil- and mineral-rich areas of Siberia) and also invade the "ancient lands that are connected with the powers of the Middle East."

This scenario regarding China truly suggests genuine veracity when the rapidly accelerating Chinese demand for oil, minerals and many other material resources is wholly contemplated. Moreover, the Chinese government and the very militant People's Liberation Army have made it very clear that they intend to replace America as the world's so-called "superpower." As one Chinese commentator adamantly proclaimed, "The twentieth century belonged to America, but this twenty-first century belongs to China!" (Incidentally, this author has been warning that China is the *real* enemy of America ever since he was forced to fight their invading hordes in North Korea in 1950, when General Douglas MacArthur had miscalculated completely China's interest in the Korean Peninsula, which truly was ironic because he had spent much of his military career in Asia and strongly believed that he understood the "inscrutable" oriental intellect and consciousness.)

As a karma-fulfilling or counterbalancing measure concerning the prophesied Chinese invasions, Dr. Hurtak's spiritual source said that China would be drastically punished for its aggressive military incursions via great suffering from the catastrophic effects of tremendous earthquakes (severe 2008 'quake) and associated inundations. This retribution would be magnified because of China's very negative karma that has been generated by its occupation of Tibet and cruel treatment of its inhabitants and also because it was responsible for the exile of its revered spiritual leader, the Dalai Lama.

Returning to the Fatima message and prophecy, the secret letter also cited the internal strife at the Vatican and within Catholicism, which in recent years has become woefully public, especially in the form of sex scandals. As the Edgar Cayce spiritual source stated, "Sex is the strongest force in man!" Indeed, it nearly induced a successful impeachment of an American president in the late 1990s.

It would appear that the most compelling reason for the Vatican not to release the contents of the Fatima message/letter could have been, and still could be, that the prophecy also included a frightening revelation that a pope would be assassinated, after which a *last* pope would be elected. Hopefully, Pope Benedict is aware of this part of the Fatima prophecy and will act accordingly.

Whereas the A.U.M. first reading of the Fatima prophecy was intended to merely satisfy the curiosity of its membership, the information in the rest of the five total readings provided philosophical enlightenment regarding the symbolism of the Marian appearances and the mission of the Christ Soul in human embodiment as Jesus/Jeshua of Nazareth.

Starting with the "Star of Bethlehem" at which the people were so captivated and awestricken at the birth of the Messiah, the Ray Stanford spiritual source revealed that this astronomical event was the result of a "rare conjunction of planets" that must have involved the brightness of Venus.

The Stanford spiritual source mentioned and explained why Jesus/Jeshua lived thirty-three (33) years in the material earth plane. Besides being symbolic of the thirty-three (33) vertebrae (at birth, and later the bones of the sacrum fuse together) in the human spinal column, this factor and number is archetypically-related to the sojourn of the Master Soul in the earth for His 33-year mission of presenting a New Covenant to humankind. Also, as previously cited, there were 33 apparitional appearances of the "angel of the Mother of Jesus" at Beauraing, Belgium. Lastly, the Perfection of Jesus/Jeshua was reached in His 33rd year of physical life following His martyrdom via crucifixion.

The total of five (5) wounds (hands, feet and torso) inflicted on the physical body of Jesus/Jeshua at the Crucifixion represented the 5 races of humankind, the 5 senses of the human body, and also the 5 children at Beauraing, whereas the 3 children at Fatima represented the Holy Trinity.

The Stanford source continued by explaining that the most spiritual number 7, as indicated in the first (Genesis) and last (Revelation) books of the Holy Bible, pertains to the 7 endocrine glands that are associated with the 7 energy centers/ chakras of the human body, and that the upper three glands (pituitary, pineal, thyroids) represent the Holy Trinity, while the four lower glands (thymus, adrenals, cells of Leydig and gonads) represent the four elements (earth, air, water and fire) of our three-dimensional material plane.

Regarding the flag of the new (1948) nation of Israel, the six-pointed star (6 is the number of responsibility and adjustments) will not be brought into perfection until there is added a seventh (7 is the number of God/Spirit) point in the center of the flag to represent the "mustard seed" of *faith* that Christ spoke of to His fellow recalcitrant Jews who are still at the consciousness level of the "imperfect 6", which is the spiritually-assigned number of Israel. This central "point" probably means that a small dot or circle needs to be added to the Israeli flag to symbolize the sun/Son of God and the Christ Light of higher consciousness! Since Jesus/Jeshua had cautioned—indeed, severely warned— the Jewish people at the Jerusalem Temple against the apparent *worship* of money and reinforced His stern remarks via the demonstrative physical act of upsetting the tables of the "money changers"(Matthew 21:12), then the fact that the new state of Israel was born with Sun in Taurus (the primary *money* sign in astrology) strongly indicates that money will continue to be a spiritual problem for the Jewish people. (Incidentally, former Jewish U.S. Federal Reserve Chairman, Alan Greenspan, having been assigned a Pisces basic personality in this incarnation, had to daily deal with huge amounts of newly-printed fiat/paper money, but the zodiacal sign of Pisces is basically a spiritual trait that generally is quite uncomfortable—Rupert Murdoch is an exception regarding other traits—when having to deal with money. Hence, the karmic/cause-and-effect indication in Mr. Greenspan's case suggests that he had been strongly averse to dealing with money in one or more past lives, or more likely, that he may have mishandled large sums of public money, and in this lifetime he dispersed it too freely.)

The Stanford source continued by explaining that Fatima, Portugal, had been chosen because it was symbolic of Mohammed's only faithful daughter, Fatima, and also that the subsequent Marian apparitions at Zeitoun, Egypt, were symbolically and spiritually connected to the original Fatima phenomena, obviously referring to the Muslim religion of Islam.

The last two Stanford readings in early 1972 pertained to additional details concerning the dire consequences that would ensue if mankind would not change its materialistic and self-centered behavior. The source of the information described *cosmic* events that were then (1972) forming *naturally,* but that would be accelerated and intensified to a physically-detrimental degree of (ionizing) radiation that would seriously deteriorate the human body. These cosmic changes may be similar to the cosmic scenario that is described in Dr. James J. Hurtak's spiritual, metaphysically-oriented book, The Book of Knowledge: The Keys of Enoch, that very scientifically depicts the entry of our solar system—and even our entire Milky Way galaxy!—into an "electromagnetic null zone." This appears to be connected with the physical electrochemical process that must occur in order for the species Homo sapiens to be metamorphosed into fifth-dimensional "whole Light beings" that will constitute the new "fifth root race" that even the Edgar Cayce spiritual source referred to in the early 1930s.

Regarding the *original* purpose for souls to experience physical embodiment and three-dimensional life in the earth plane, about six years before the A.U.M. membership received the Fatima prophecy readings a detailed discourse concerning the Creation was presented via the Stanford psychic source. It stated that souls originally entered the earth plane apparently while in their natural etheric form as "thought forms", just as the Edgar Cayce spiritual source had mentioned many decades previously. However, the Stanford source provided a more detailed account and elucidation concerning both the incipient Creation and the subsequent evolution of the species Homo sapiens, including the real spiritual and physical nature of the Christ Soul as Amelius, and also His evolving purpose and mission as a Guiding Consciousness concerning the Divine Plan for the spiritual evolutionary process for what was to become a human being and later our present Adamic race. Both the evolutionists and creationists are only partly correct in their philosophy and anthropology regarding the lineage of humankind, especially concerning the anthropoid ape of which the Stanford source more correctly termed a "proanthropoid" life form. Also, there was no *transition* from ape to a human form because the original entrance or migration of souls into matter occurred when the etheric souls merely entered and assimilated the physical bodies of the proanthropoids as a willful desire to experience this form of expression. The souls at that time (just as in the present regarding a human baby) possessed the power to enter in and also exit any form of matter. However, many souls intensely enjoyed their new physical form, obviously the gratifying sexual aspect, and eventually became trapped in these proanthropoids and other forms of physical life, and soul memories of these pleasant physical experiences continued for a long period following the inception of the new distinct and separate present Adamic race as a special soul evolutionary vehicle that was initiated with the entrance of the Christ Soul as Adam (the "Son of man", as Jesus/ Jeshua correctly referred to Himself).

126

Indeed, even up to the time of the construction of the Sphinx in Egypt (*before* the Great Pyramid was built) some human beings still were being born with *tails* (consider the coccyx or tail bone as the lower terminus of the human spinal column), and this anatomical aberration is still occurring in a developmental stage in human babies to this date. Those wall drawings of human-animal life forms in Egypt were depicting actual human anatomical conditions! The Edgar Cayce spiritual source said that when Cayce himself had been Ra Ta in Egypt at the time of the construction of the Great Pyramid, he had helped many of these unfortunate entities to become normal human beings, and in this present lifetime he would continue his humanitarian endeavor via his practice as a psychic medical diagnostician. His assignment—and acceptance—of a Pisces Sun Sign (basic character) was very harmonious and augmentative for such an intuitive activity, albeit his assigned number 8 material-oriented life path/lesson (per natal numeroscope) indicated that he would have to struggle with money problems, and he even lost his beloved hospital during the Great Depression, which had been a gift from a grateful person who had received many psychic readings.

Both the Stanford spiritual source and the Edgar Cayce spiritual source agree regarding the initiation of a Divine Plan that was devised as the proper and necessary method for *perfecting* the renegade, willful souls that had gotten mired in physical animal form, and this most likely applies also to those souls who had been led astray by Lucifer, the false Light who had instigated and perpetrated the "revolt in heaven." This is the same Satan that tested Jesus/Jeshua for forty (prime testing number 40) days and nights immediately following His baptism by John the Baptist, and also who all of us can be tempted by at our weakest spiritual consciousness times, as Christ warned. This Divine Plan appointed the volunteering Master Christ Soul as first a "hovering" Consciousness Guide during the animal fiasco and later in physical embodiment as the ruler Amelius of the *red* race that was assigned to the continent of Atlantis (Atlantic Ocean area versus the *yellow* race in the continent of Lemuria/ Mu that was located in the area of the Pacific Ocean). Much later, the corruption, greed and intense materialism (like today in the world) of the Atlanteans that had manifested via human free will and self-centeredness, along with their technological achievements such as the powerful "firestone" that had harnessed the sun's energy, combined in the massive destruction of Atlantis. This same Amelius had created the charts and calendars that much later most likely became known as the Tzolkin (Mayan Sacred Calendar) when the Atlantean refugees took these charts and calendars to the Yucatan Peninsula, according to the Cayce source, and they even built the first pyramid in that area, indicating that the peoples called the Maya, Aztec and Inca really were the refugees and descendants of the red race of Atlantis, as proposed in Chapter 5. The destruction and submergence of the antediluvian continents of Atlantis and Lemuria/Mu most likely had been connected with the Great Flood in Genesis, which would have caused the deaths (soul transition) of most of the world's human population.

The Christ Soul was sent to Earth to initiate our present Adamic race, and this was to be followed by periodic future incarnations to function as a continuing Source of guidance concerning the Divine Plan, and these subsequent earthly visitations included Enoch, Melchizedek and Jesus/Jeshua. Whether His arrival in the earth plane was via biological or metaphysical processes, the Christ Soul tried to raise the consciousness of human beings during each of these earthly visitations, and the final phase (2012?) obviously is intended to transform the human brain/mind to the highest level of a Cosmic Consciousness.

CHAPTER 8

The Number 17 and the Evolutionary Process of the United States of America

To reiterate solely for the purpose of this chapter, the number 17 is first specifically and dramatically cited in the very first book of the Holy Bible where it pertains to the beginning day of the massive, purging, human-eradicating Flood, and this number 17 also is strangely cited as the specific day when Noah's huge ark/ship mercifully grounded on a mountain in Ararat. Hence, the number 17 obviously pertains to both *suffering* and *redemption*, and we may assume that the long time period of many months that Noah and his family endured on that floating vessel represents the number 17 also, which, symbolically, should indicate the long spiritual evolutionary process of humankind that appears to be nearing its culmination (2012?).

To reiterate further solely for emphasis of the number 17 concerning this very specific chapter, pyramidologists have noticed that the unusual, odd number 17 is the key number regarding the basic message and theme of the Great Pyramid because the so-called "displacement factor" of 286.1 pyramid inches reduces and vibrates to the very important biblical number 17, and even the chronological ending date for the Pyramid was September 17, 2001! Moreover, the number 17 becomes the most important number of the Pythagorean Divine Triangle (Life Theorem) when it is interpreted *wholistically*, and, albeit only presented indirectly, it is revealed to be the most important spiritual number that is associated with the seemingly enigmatic act by Christ (see John 21:11) wherein this Master Metaphysician "deposited" 153 (total of the numerals 1 through 17 and also 9 x 17) fish in the net for the disciples just prior to His final Ascension.

The number 17 is heavily involved with the conception and birth of the United States of America, and also its process of evolution concerning its ultimate destiny that is surprisingly depicted in Dr. James J. Hurtak's supremely metaphysically-oriented and obviously very spiritual book, The Book of Knowledge: The Keys of Enoch, which expands and magnifies the full scope of spiritual science.

Whereas the number 17 involves the continuing evolutionary process for America, the very spiritual numbers 13 and 50 pertain primarily to the form and geographical structure of the country because it began as a confederation of 13 individual colonies/states with separate, distinct governing bodies that now has expanded to the *final* (Puerto Rico will never become a state of America) 50 collective—but very *individual*—unique states.

Historians have speculated and informed the American public that many of the founding fathers, especially its prominent figurehead, George Washington, were active members of the fraternal organization known as Freemasonry, and the unusual features of the Great Seal of the United States appear to confirm this supposition and claim, especially regarding the obviously high consciousness and uniqueness of the founding fathers. Since the Edgar Cayce spiritual source spoke of the entry of "group souls" into embodiment in the earth plane concerning a specific, important human task that they all desired intensely to perform, it is likely that this may have been the situation regarding the dedicated founding fathers of the United States of America. A thorough knowledge and understanding of the immutable spiritual law of cause-and-effect/karma should induce plausibility in this case.

The Great Seal design was transferred to the currency/legal tender of America, and the truncated pyramid, with its 13 courses of masonry (representing the 13 states) and its Eye of Providence and Osiris that replaces the missing capstone of the Great Pyramid, are truly unusual features since the United States of America is so distant from Egypt and its ideology and primary religion. However, the pyramid symbol is quite harmonious with the ideology and philosophy of Freemasonry. The number 13 is indirectly displayed all over the dollar bill and the Great Seal regarding the total number of stars, arrows, stripes and olive leaves, and it seems revealing (from a spiritual evolutionary perspective) that there are 9—not the pervasive, omnipresent 13—feathers on the tail of the eagle.

The Latin words, ANNUIT COEPTIS (He hath prospered our beginnings), contain 13 letters, and the words, E PLURIBUS UNUM (one out of many, i.e., one union of 13 states), also contain 13 letters. However, the auspicious, grandiose, presumptuous words, NOVUS ORDO SECLORUM (a new order of the ages), contain the most important and special number 17 that is derived from the total of letters in this declaration. It probably is significant that these dramatic words are placed at the base of the unfinished pyramid because America very obviously is still in an evolutionary process that the period 2000–2008 (Bush "Administration") has illustrated so painfully to the world, but the 2008 number 1 world year of new beginnings will change everything completely for America.

The importance of the number 50 for America relates to its final expansion to a total of fifty (50) individual, self-governing states, even though the two added states (Alaska and Hawaii) are not part of the contiguous forty-eight (48) states. As cited previously in this book, the number 50 is called the Pythagorean Sacred Number, and it also applies to the vertical location of the so-called King's Chamber at the fiftieth (50) course of masonry/ blocks in the Great Pyramid. This final expansion to fifty (50) unionized individual states suggests that America could be nearing the ending process of its obviously predestined purpose, mission and *destiny*!

The concept of a collective union of the thirteen colonies probably first was considered seriously at the Albany Congress in New York in 1754, which was a number 17 world year. Actually, the number 17 was first associated with the evolution and destiny of America in 1619 (another number 17 world year) when the original colony of Jamestown in Virginia established its first representative government, but this colony basically pertained to merely a *business* proposition, especially regarding the abomination of tobacco. Contrarily, the religious, freedom-seeking Pilgrims arrived in the new world of America in 1620, which was a number 9 world year that basically pertains to endings, but here it may have involved the number 9 destiny of humankind. Of course, it was the ending of the old European form of Christianity that the Vatican in Rome had imposed so forcefully and ignorantly, thereby virtually coercing free-thinking Christians like Martin Luther to become Protestants.

Regarding the American Revolutionary War that established the United States of America as a new sovereign world nation and power, the number 17 was profoundly instrumental during this war for independence. If the British had known and understood the full meaning and significance of the number 17 and its association with the destiny of America and its disastrous numerical vibration for them, they never would have fought any major battle on any number 17 day, as the following crucial military engagements of the American Revolutionary War convincingly illustrate:

> 1. The Battle of Bunker Hill (Breed's Hill) occurred on June 17, 1775. The British suffered the loss of almost half of their attacking force during repeated stupid, massed, frontal assaults, but which comprised the

traditional military modus operandi at that time, and that eventually destroyed Napoleon's massive army, but the Russian winter was really the coup de grace.

2. The Battle of Boston (actually a winter siege) lasted nine (the number 9 of endings and the human destiny number) months and ended on March 17, 1776, when British ships finally arrived to evacuate their military forces and many Tories and relocate them to Canada.

3. The Battle of Saratoga was the first large, decisive military engagement of the war in which the British surrendered on October 17, 1777, following a series of skirmishes and battles. Like the U.S. Civil War's major, 3-day Battle of Gettysburg in 1863 (=18 time number) this large battle proved to be the turning point of the war because it enlisted the aid of France by proving that the Americans really could defeat their arch nemesis, England. [Incidentally, this battle was fought during July 1,2 and 3 (3 is the whole number), and was an unintentional large battle that intervened with and interrupted supreme Confederate General Robert E. Lee's plan to capture Washington, D.C. It should be ironically noteworthy that Lee retreated back to the South on July 4th, which was the anniversary of America's Independence Day.]

4. The Battle of Cowpens ended the British series of successes in the South when the American victory on January 17, 1781, forced the British to withdraw to the seaport town of Yorktown in Virginia.

5. The Battle of Yorktown began as a siege that included brief skirmishes that ended when General Cornwallis *capitulated* on October 17, 1781. However, the formal surrender "ceremony" did not occur until two days later on October 19 because of the reluctance of the great Lord Cornwallis to meet with the rebel General Washington regarding this ignominious defeat,

and perhaps also because many French soldiers formed a large segment of the conquering army. Indeed, Cornwallis would not meet with George Washington until October 27 (number of big endings), which truly signified that this had been the last major battle of the entire war. Moreover, 1781 was a number 17 world year that may have involved British negative karma. However, the war continued on at sea (consider hero Captain John Paul Jones) until 1783, which was a number 1 world year of new beginnings, and the Treaty of Paris was signed to finally end the long war in its ninth (9) year, and here the number 9 may have involved both an ending indicator and the destiny number of humankind. (Incidentally, this same seaport town, Yorktown, was again under a month-long siege by Union forces during the American Civil War in 1862, which was another number 17 world year!).

On September 17, 1787, following four (4 is a basic testing number) years of frustrating political arguments, the thirteen (13) now united states finally signed their new Constitution of the United States of America. The seventeenth (17) day of the month is significant enough (regarding the Book of Genesis in the Holy Bible), but the numerical vibration for this momentous year is the same number 5 as the birth date vibration for America ($1+7+8+7 = 23 = 5$ and $7+4+1+7+7+6 = 32 = 5$), and the number 5 pertains to freedom, independence, change, as well as being the *number* of man. Moreover, the birth of America occurred during the more astrologically potent middle decanate of the zodiacal sign of Cancer, which is strongly associated with the home and family and all familial activties. Hence, the domain of homes/houses and all real estate matters is of primary concern to Americans, and the present (2006–2008) "mortgage meltdown" regarding lending institutions testifies to an excessive concern with home ownership that was perpetuated by the greed of these bankers.

Apparently, the next major event concerning the number 17 and the evolutionary process of America occurred when the seventeenth (17) president of the United States of America, Andrew Johnson, became the first president to be impeached, and merely one vote saved him from his removal from this high office. The second and last (to date) U.S.A. president to experience the humiliating, ignominious ordeal of impeachment was William (Bill) Clinton, and this involved merely a minor personal sexual indiscretion that induced him to lie to his revengeful interrogators. Again, the number 17 figured prominently and conspicuously throughout the entire lengthy impeachment process. (Incidentally, albeit the exact birth time for America has not been ascertained, some astrologers make a good case for assigning the zodiacal sign of Scorpio as America's ascendant/ rising sign, which appears to be accurate when evaluating and pondering America's preoccupation and unnatural attitude about sex in any form. Many of its public "servants", from clergy to federal government, have committed sexual acts that proved their utter hypocrisy concerning sexual mores and behavior. The sign of Scorpio is connected to the solar 8th house that has a strong sexual component and trait regarding regeneration and rebirth. Also, if Japan and Germany had understood the revenge aspects of Scorpio, it seems likely that they never would have attacked Scorpionic America—"Don't Tread On Me!")

It seems ironic and grossly unfair that America's current (2000-2008) president has made a mockery of the internationally-envied U.S. Constitution by attempts to circumvent its legislative contents and the overall spirit of its almost holy nature. Concerning at least a psychological purpose, the extremely freedom-loving New England state of Vermont has voted to impeach President George W. Bush, who has initiated an immoral, unjust war in Iraq, bankrupted the U.S.A., deceived 60,000,000 members of the electorate—twice!—by falsely magnifying their extreme fear of terrorists, and incited the wrath and enmity of many global countries. Therefore, regarding an impeachment justification, he has made Andrew Johnson and Bill Clinton to appear as virtual angels.

Hopefully, America in 2009 quickly can atone for and dissipate its extremely negative, recently-produced karma in reference to its hegemonic, imperialistic and militaristic global behavior with its aggressive, self-perpetuating, dominating actions that have incited the enmity and disdain of many sovereign countries in the world, including those that formerly had admired America as the bulwark of true democracy. Indeed, the American federal government during the period 2000–2008 virtually has been controlled and dominated by a triumvirate that essentially has transformed it into an oligarchy. The spiritual sciences of numerology and astrology strongly indicate that this unholy situation and condition will end in 2008, regardless of the fact that this is a presidential election year for America. The number 1 world year of 2008 itself will assure that new beginnings (hopefully positive) will occur for the entire world.

Astrologically, the recent entry of both Pluto (transformation and consciousness) and giant Jupiter (expansion, but even to an excessive degree such as the current credit and currency crisis) into the extremely earthy and materialistic zodiacal sign of Capricorn virtually assures that the present American government "leadership" will be completely replaced, and this also applies to many world governments and their present rulers, just as Dr. Carl Johan Calleman's spiritual interpretation of the Mayan Sacred Calendar/Tzolkin indicates.

To mitigate somewhat this author's seemingly austere indictment of the entity known as George W. Bush, the spiritual science of astrology should provide a modicum of understanding regarding the truly sincere behavior of this U.S. president. Like America, he was born with Sun in Cancer and its strongest middle decanate. This basic Cancer personality strongly induces him to be a home-loving, nurturing, emotional person, and this is indicated via his irresistible urge to spend as much time as possible at his ranch in Texas, where he often invites world leaders and where he (obviously unconsciously) deceived Russian President Putin, and his primary, partner-seeking Libra personality. The strong Cancer traits indicate that the hastily-formed, fear-driven Department of Homeland Security is one of the main concerns for George Bush, but the monetary expense of this behemoth has contributed greatly to the bankruptcy of America. Of course, this financial condition already had been assured by the Iraq war that is really doomed to failure because the accelerated initial attack was perpetrated on March 19, 2003 (date vibrates to the time number 18), while Sun still was activating the zodiacal sign of Pisces (solar 12th house of self-undoing), thereby indicating that this war would be merely a Pyrrhic victory (not worth the cost in time, money and human lives).

To continue with this astrological character assessment of George Bush and his qualifications for leadership of a great country, his ascendant/rising sign (outer personality) is Leo, which induces him to truly believe that he is the world's greatest leader, however megalomaniacal this self-perception is for him. It truly hurts him emotionally (strong Cancer trait) when the whole world does not acknowledge this unique feature and dares to criticize his sincere behavior. Tragically and dangerously, Leo is a *fire* sign and Cancer is a *water* sign, and this combination can build up steam pressure, thus giving him a tendency to at least figuratively "blow himself up", especially regarding his massive Leo ego. The Leo personality is very susceptible to flattery, which could lead even to megalomania, and this also would apply to the extremely popular 2008 presidential candidate, Barack Obama, whose Sun is in Leo. His female opponent, Hillary Clinton, has a strong Scorpio personality and truly could be relied on to practice patience, persistence and perseverance to "get the job done", and her compassionate Pisces Moon Sign (emotional makeup) would assure that she would do her utmost in her sincere attempts to provide health care and sustenance for the ailing masses of people. Indeed, no presidential candidate should be selected without a thorough evaluation of his/her natal horoscope, as the Edgar Cayce spiritual source advised when it stated: "It would be well for *everyone* to study astrology." The source quickly added that we should be certain to "do it right!"

Having previously mentioned the intensely freedom-loving American state of Vermont, the number 17 was quite prominent regarding the front-running, 2004 Democratic presidential candidate, Vermont Governor Howard Dean, who was born on November 17 (another Scorpio who would have quickly straightened out the messes that George Bush had created during his first disastrous term). Albeit being the initial leading candidate who had been expected to easily receive the Democratic nomination, according to the news media reports he lost the first seventeen (17) presidential primaries and caucuses before quitting the contest. The last of these contests was on February 17, and he officially terminated his candidacy on February 18 (the *time* number). Tragically, if the American electorate had studied, evaluated and understood that his Sun in Scorpio, when combined with his domestic, nurturing, family-oriented Cancer ascendant/rising sign, should have presented America with a fine, effective president, as well as a *medical doctor*. Additionally, both his Scorpio Sun and Cancer ascendant would have been very harmonious with the natal horoscope of the U.S.A. Moreover, any Scorpio presidential candidate of any political party would have a distinct advantage of being elected president because the primary influence of Sun in Scorpio and his/her solar first house of new beginnings would offer tremendous assistance for success on election day, and this would explain why America has had so many Scorpio presidents. Hence, until the American electorate utilizes the very useful assistance of astrology, they obviously will continue to make the wrong choices that can result in another grossly-ignorant and very disastrous national leader like George W. Bush.

Returning to the number 17 and its strong association with the evolution of America, during the U.S. Civil War the first Union military victory occurred at Antietam Creek, near Sharpsburg, Maryland, on September 17, 1862, which also was a number 17 world year (1+8+6+2). This truly was a day of *suffering* for both the North and the South, since it proved to have been the bloodiest one-day battle of the entire Civil War. Nonetheless, President Abraham Lincoln had been impatiently awaiting a Union victory so as to officially and publicly present his momentous Emancipation Proclamation concerning the abomination of slavery, so he reluctantly decided to use this Pyrrhic victory to publicly present the document on January 1, 1863, which was both a number 1 day of new beginnings and also a *time* number 18 world year. Later, the 13th (!) Amendment to the U.S. Constitution finally terminated the ugly stigma of slavery that had manifested so much negative karma that it necessitated the sacrifice of over half a million American lives to dissipate the accumulated karma to that point in time. Of course, the horrendous treatment of the "native Americans", especially the Cherokee death march, would begin generating much more negative karma, but perhaps the human losses of World War I and World War II served to dissipate at least some of that negative karma.

The American Civil War *effectively* ended with the surrender of General Robert E. Lee's army on April 9 (number of endings) in 1865. General Lee issued General Order #9 (endings) to his soldiers, which instructed them to lay down their arms and to disband without resorting to guerilla warfare.

America was still in the process of attaining its "manifest destiny" when it deliberately provoked a war with Spain in 1898

139

under the pretext of altruistically trying to help the persecuted inhabitants of Cuba. Using what apparently since has been proven to have been an accidental explosion (gunpowder stored too close to the steam boilers) on the battleship U.S.S. Maine in Havana harbor as just cause, America demanded that Spain withdraw its army from Cuba. Obviously being very aware of its role as a world colonial power, Spain then quickly reciprocated by declaring war on America, just as America had hoped and planned. The ensuing rapid American military response and actions on both land and sea resulted in the destruction of the Spanish fleets at the Philippines and at Cuba. The disastrous land and sea defeats at Santiago, Cuba, induced Spanish General Toral to *capitulate* on July 17 (!), albeit the official surrender by the Spanish government occurred on July 18 (the *time* number), which was a situation similar to the British surrender at Yorktown in 1781. Hence, the Spanish-American War catapulted America onto the global stage as a dominant world power, and it has exercised this power ever since then, which further indicates that Scorpio is America's ascendant/rising sign, astrologically, because a primary trait of this zodiacal sign induces the entity to strongly desire to take control and to maintain control in any situation that requires a return to stability and *order*. (Incidentally, this is why Scorpio Hillary Rodham Clinton truly believes that her *destiny* and duty is to become president of the totally-disorganized dis-United States of America, and her various planets in the sign of Scorpio serve to intensify and magnify this desire. Truly, this unique, remarkable woman would dedicate herself completely to restoring America and returning it to its real purpose and *destiny* that should be directly associated with its predestined spiritual path. Moreover, Hillary Clinton, at age 60, is still experiencing the powerful destiny effects of her second Saturn Return, astrologically, and at the soul/superconscious level she *knows* that now is the time for her to persist in her attempt to become the leader of America and the "free world.")

Regarding the Apollo Space Program for exploration of Earth's moon, Apollo 13 (!) was launched in 1970 (=17), but the mission had to be aborted before its scheduled moon landing because of a ruptured oxygen tank. The anxious crew had to use the power and survival system of the Lunar Landing Module to return to Earth, and they "splashed down" on April 17 (!) You can be certain that the NASA scientists were questioning their seemingly defiant application of the sequential number 13 during those seven harrowing days of the ordeal. However, we need to concede and sympathize with any scientist who does not want to be labeled as being superstitious or even a victim of *triskaidekaphobia* (fear of the number 13).

Some other notable number 17 factors and incidents that were and are involved in the vicissitudes and evolutionary process of America are:

1. Both founding fathers and U.S. presidents John Adams and Thomas Jefferson returned to the realm of Spirit on the same day at nearly the same time, and it truly is amazing that this particular—predestined?—date was July 4, 1826. This was not only the anniversary of America's Declaration of Independence (July 4, 1776), but 1826 was a number 17 world year (1+8+2+6). Albeit John Adams was much older than Jefferson, they both lived exactly 50 (American key number) years to the day from when Jefferson's Declaration of Independence was signed by the founding fathers.

2. The Cuban Bay of Pigs disastrous invasion attempt on April 17 in the number 17 world year of 1961. This was a Florida-based, CIA-directed, Cuban refugee operation to depose Fidel Castro and that the U.S. military would not support because a newly-installed,

neophyte U.S. president was too apprehensive and fearful of retaliation by the Soviet Union concerning its strategic satellite that was only about 90 miles from its arch enemy, America, in defiance of the Monroe Doctrine.

3. The two most recent highly-destructive California earthquakes occurred on October 17, 1989 (even a number 27 world year of big endings), near San Francisco, and January 17, 1994, near Los Angeles. Ironically, the next large, highly-destructive earthquake occurred on the same day (January 17) one year later at Kobe, Japan—the so-called "rule of three" to satisfy the *whole* number 3?

4. The official income tax instruction book of the Internal Revenue Service (?) is Publication 17!

5. A widespread California electrical blackout occurred on January 17, 2001, which was on the anniversary of the January 17, 1994, costly earthquake.

6. The American World War II heavy bomber, the B-17 Flying Fortress, suffered horrendous, grievous human losses concerning both its crew members and the German people. The aeronautical engineers at the Boeing Airplane Company obviously had no awareness or understanding of the full meaning and purpose of the number 17.

7. Just after departing from New York City, Flight 800 (extreme material number) exploded on July 17, 1996, returning 230 souls to the realm of Spirit.

8. On February 17, 2009, all owners and users of analog-type television sets will be coerced to convert to the newer replacement digital system, and they will have to purchase a converter box.

9. The trajectory of the rifle bullet that killed President John F. Kennedy was at 17 degrees (actually 17 degrees, 43 minutes and 30 seconds, and these added numerals, 1+7+4+3+3+0, vibrate to the *time*

number 18). Karma suggests that in a past life he had assassinated a notable public person.

10. The U.S. Democratic Party held 17 presidential candidate debates in January, 2008 (number 1 world year of new beginnings), that involved an unusually large group of candidates that resulted in the obvious supremacy of only two contestants, viz., a white *woman* and a *semi-black* (bi-racial or mulatto) man. This situation was unparalleled in the entire history of America, but this social condition correlates perfectly with Dr. Carl Johan Calleman's spiritual interpretation of the Mayan Sacred Calendar/Tzolkin that Chapter 5 indicates originated from the Christ Soul and probably was updated by the Christ disciple, Didymos Thomas, when he was Quetzalcoatl. Since Dr. Calleman's "World Tree" is now in the process of undergoing a complete, 180-degree reversal concerning all mental and material concerns, then the above political situation becomes quite understandable, thereby indicating that now is the *time* for America to elect either a qualified white female or even a *fully* black person to become its president. From a spiritual law of cause-and-effect/karmic standpoint, much of America's prodigious black-African negative karma certainly was dissipated via the loss of over one-half million lives in the Civil War, so it would appear that the installation of a white female as the nation's president is warranted. Alas, whoever becomes America's next president on January 20, 2009, certainly will face the most difficult national and international situations and conditions of *any* prior U.S. president. Moreover, 2009 will be a number 11 world year, indicating that there will be serious relationship misunderstandings between the nations of the world. Think Fatima prophecy!

143

Since greed, corruption and materialism have become rampant in America and the world now, perhaps it might be interesting to speculate as to the *real* meaning of why in recent years the American retail-pricing system concerning consumer products has been changed from its long-time practice of applying a decimal of 95 cents to 99 cents, such as $1.95 to $1.99, ostensibly indicating extreme greed. Hopefully, this relatively-recent, double-nine pricing was motivated subconsciously from Spirit to manifest a number 9 consciousness, just as the present global proliferation of the number 9-oriented, brain-taxing game of Sudoku may have been motivated from Spirit. Realistically, the prophecy of Christ (see Matthew 24) sadly indicates that this increased squeezing of the dollar was solely or primarily done to produce as much profit as possible from the purchased item, thereby indicating that the "last days" of the Piscean Age have arrived and their dire scenario activated.

An intentional deviation from the cited primary numbers of this chapter (13, 17, 18, 27 and 50) probably is necessary to conclude this numerological study of America because the identifying number of the presidential White House in Washington is 1600. This unusual number has biblical ramifications, as cited in Revelation 14:20 of the very last book of the Holy Bible, albeit basically applied as a number of measurement in John's complex vision. However, at least one theologian's research has indicated that the number 1600 is associated with "Divine Judgment", marking events as "Divine pressures" are applied to *faulty* institutions and procedures of materialistic humanity. Any development that serves to intensify the ordeal of world judgment may be marked by this factor. Thus, can there be a more applicable *"faulty institution"* at this time than the U.S. presidential White House with its intrigue and immoral, disastrous Iraq blunder, and its extreme global complications and consequences? Spiritual laws dictate that we must *reap* what we sow, and no one, not even gigantic, mighty America and its self-serving, grossly-inept president and his deluded sycophants, can circumvent or escape the judgment of the immutable law of cause-and-effect, regardless of how sincere such purpose and actions may have been intended. Even the judicial laws of humankind tend not to excuse the condition of *ignorance*.

The theologian author of the above pronouncement further stated that this number 1600 also signifies "fullness of chastisement" because of the significance of the factors that make up this number (40 x 40 = 1600, and 40 is an extreme *testing* number all throughout the Holy Bible, and in this American situation and application this testing number is even *squared*).

Some Bible scholars and theologians are convinced that some of the early American founders and immigrants were descendants of the dispersed and "lost" tribes of Israel and Judah. Indeed, even the Edgar Cayce spiritual source back in the 1930s revealed that members of these "lost" tribes had arrived from Asia by ships to settle at the coastal areas of the western hemisphere, primarily in Central and South America, where Jewish/Hebrew artifacts and evidence have been discovered by archeologists. Hence, it follows that if the Anglo-Saxon peoples included the dispersed and wandering Jews and Israelites, then the number 17 aptly fits the pervasiveness of this number of suffering and redemption in all of the activities of America. Moreover, since Jesus/Jeshua (the true Messiah) had warned His fellow Jews that they had a serious *money* problem, perhaps it is obvious why America is so preoccupied with money, business and profits, as the world's financial capital, New York City (Wall Street), dramatically indicates. Indeed, a primary, consistent topic on the evening news of the three (whole number again) major television networks, ABC, CBS and NBC, concerns the daily activities of the New York stock exchanges. Additionally, this further would serve to explain why America is so inextricably tied to Israel, no matter what the cost, especially via exorbitant monetary loans, which really are "gifts." Moreover, this powerful, Arab/Muslim-detesting alliance and inseperable partnership strongly indicates that the scenario for the seemingly imminent third world war that is depicted in the Fatima prophecy may be imminent, especially regarding the nuclear aspirations of Iran and the Israeli determination that their perpetuation of this matter will not be tolerated.

A final interesting and corroborating American situation that in January, 2008, appeared to be approaching a climactic point, involved the Jehovah-ordered practice of circumcision that the patriarch, Abraham, was instructed to perform on himself and every male member of the Hebrew tribes. The news media reported details of the continuing controversy concerning the dubious necessity of circumcising American babies soon after their birth, which obviously still is a customary Jewish practice in the world that the Germans successfully utilized as a rapid means for identifying Jews. Of course, the obvious reason that Jehovah/God/Creative Forces demanded circumcision involved physical hygiene and sexually transmitted diseases, which is why African men are enduring the painful after-effects of this surgical procedure that they hope will prevent incubation of the HIV precursor of AIDS.

CHAPTER 9

Numerological and Astrological Influences on World Economics

Regarding most past, present and future major global events, economic or otherwise, a sufficient amount of objective investigation and research into the two primary spiritual sciences should reveal that numerological and astrological influences were, are and will be at least contributing factors concerning cause and effect. However, all conditions cannot be attributed to metaphysics because the human birthright of *free will* can, and often does, supersede or override every other factor involved in any physical, emotional and material situation, such as the airplane destruction of the World Trade Towers in New York City by Islamic religious extremists. Nonetheless, more often than not, numerical and planetary vibrational energies—everything is in a constant state of vibration, whether atomic or etheric—do have a significant influence, sometimes to a catastrophic degree, depending on human responses and subsequent actions.

The year 2007, having been an especially important number 9 world year of *endings*, is a prime example because it proved to have been perhaps the worst (albeit 2008 may be even worse) financial year in America's economic history, and the economic events of 2008 should reveal the magnitude of the disaster involving the once-mighty U.S. dollar. In November, 2007, with Sun in Scorpio (signifying death and rebirth), the dollar-value index fell to a 230-year low. Actually, the exact date that the demise of the U.S. dollar was initiated occurred on September 27, 2007, which was supremely significant and revealing because it showed that this specific date really formed a *triplication* of the number 9, being the ninth (9) month, and the year 2007 vibrates to 9 also. Not only does the 27th day equal 9, but it again is a triplication of the number 9, while the number 27 itself pertains to big endings. Is it any wonder why the financial world, especially China, is becoming increasingly reluctant to accept the U.S. dollar as a "stable anchor in the global financial system?" As of this writing in July of 2008, U.S. Federal Reserve Chairman "Helicopter Ben" Bernanke is continuing to throw out billions of newly-printed fiat dollars to large—make that *huge*—bankrupt financial lending institutions in an desperate attempt—it's really too late—to save the corrupt American banking system, economy and stock markets, but it appears that the billions—no, *trillions*—of dollars that have been"invested" in *derivatives* (actually bets and debts) may/ will eventually stretch the global financial system beyond its elastic limit, resulting in catastrophic failure, just as the Mayan calendar appears to indicate. Some financial analysts have called the domain of derivatives the "Grand Casino", which depicts the ultimate gambling nature of this looming nightmare.

The severe devaluation of the U.S. currency inexorably will increase greatly the rate of inflation, which the unfortunate Federal Reserve Chairman Bernanke—Alan Greenspan made his exit just in time—is virtually forced to endure because the gang at the White House and the Secretary of the Treasury are very aware that 2008 is a critical election year in which the American electorate is determined to end the nightmare of the Bush regime. Financially, America is now experiencing a classic Catch-22 situation. Expressed plainly, this means "damned if we do and damned if we don't."

Another convincing numerological indicator that American supremacy in the global financial system is being terminated, including its own financial system, is the fact that in 2007 (number 9 year of endings) the U.S. national debt reached a staggering $9 trillion dollars—yes, that is 9 with 12 zeroes! The crucial number 9 indicates that a debt this huge assures an ending scenario, and it also is the *cyclic* number for humankind. The cyclic number 9 in this case is singularly significant because it was in 1998 that the U.S.A. and the world barely avoided a financial meltdown (key nuclear age word). Not only was this nine (9) years before 2007 (one cycle), but it was a number 27 (triplication of the number 9) world year of big endings, and later in this chapter the year 1998 will be discussed, examined and compared with the mysterious number 666 in the Book of Revelation of the Holy Bible. To reinforce the significance of the $9 trillion national debt, the recent amount of plastic debt that American consumers have generated and accumulated is approximately 900 billion dollars, which, numerologically, indicates that this credit card debt will result in a large number of personal bankruptcies, just when a recently-enacted bankruptcy law induces greater hardships on those being forced into this humiliating experience and when inflationary pressures are accelerating. The accompanying home mortgage foreclosures are driving real estate prices down sharply from the dizzying height at which they never would have attained if the greedy, devious mortgage bankers and the real estate speculators had been regulated by the government. This collective scenario is verifying the accuracy and validity of the spiritually-oriented predictions for the ending of the (Piscean) Age, especially as Christ described it.

Having begun this chapter by citing the deteriorating condition of the American economy, the involvement of America's special number 17 should be noted. The news media, while reporting governmental economic statistics for the year of 2007, mentioned two economic indicators that had just reached 17-year lows, one of which pertained to the worst consumer price inflation in seventeen (17) years. Continuing with the bad news that also included the observation that the *median* price of U.S. homes had declined for the first time since the Great Depression, it also was revealed that 17,000 jobs had been lost in

January, 2008 (the month just prior to this news report), whereas an *increase* in employment had been expected. The *actual* inflation rate for 2007 was quoted as 17% for the U.S., which was much higher than the extremely deceptive, so-called *core* inflation rate that intentionally does not include food, energy and transportation costs, which is totally ludicrous.

Not to be neglected and omitted, the number 27 of big endings also moved onto center stage when it was revealed that new homebuilding activity had sunk to a 27-year low, but gold (the best form of *real* money, albeit silver is one of the best bargains in the world because it is such a precious, necessary commodity and is currently priced so low) had attained a 27-year high in price in the 2007 number 9 world year of endings. Even silver, the "poor man's gold", reached a 27-year high in value in January, 2008, which is a number 1 world year of new beginnings. The global financial and economic pattern strongly indicates that the prices/values of gold, silver and all other *natural* resources will appreciate far beyond mostly everyone's expectations because of greatly increased and accelerating consumer consumption, especially concerning the surging Asian economies with their approximately three billion people who fervently desire to establish a more luxurious lifestyle such as the West (especially America) has enjoyed for the past century.

Concerning astrological influences and the global economy, the increasingly-high prices of food, gasoline, crude oil, heating oil and natural gas during 2007 should have made most or all of the consumers in the world very pessimistic. Contrarily, the transits of Jupiter and Pluto in Sagittarius would have engendered undue optimism in the psyche of humans, inducing a feeling and belief that this depressing condition merely would be a temporary hardship that soon would be mitigated, just as always had occurred previously for most of them. Actually, this euphoria had been manifesting since Pluto (consciousness) had first entered the very optimistic zodiacal sign of Sagittarius in 1995, and Jupiter (expansive) also in this same sign for that first year added impetus and emphasis. This is why the 1990s produced perhaps the best economic decade of the twentieth century, and why U.S. President Bill Clinton (1992–2000) was able to balance the federal budget. Albeit the negative component of Sagittarius, which pertains to religion and philosophy, obviously initiated the rise of Islamic extremism, the positive aspect induced a strong interest in metaphysics and the "New Age" philosophy, which produced a proliferation of literature. Regarding economics, this would help to explain why the world did not suffer a financial collapse during the global monetary crisis in 1998 because the "collective unconscious" would have generated sufficient optimism to negate a catastrophe. Also, it was late in this period (1995–2007) that U.S. Federal Reserve Chairman Alan Greenspan had uttered his now famous expression, "irrational exuberance" (Sagittarius effect), when he appeared before the U.S. Congress to define the booming economic conditions in America.

Now that Pluto has begun (late January, 2008) its lengthy transit of the serious material and business zodiacal sign of Capricorn, the global collective unconscious should engender a more realistic appraisal and pragmatic attitude toward the material aspects of life and business in general. The 2008 added presence of gigantic Jupiter in this same sign of Capricorn should magnify and expand the material concerns of humankind, especially regarding personal sustenance and survival, and thereby diminishing some of the spiritual gains that had been produced during 1995–2007. Many people will be trying to start a new business, but most likely because they have lost their regular employment and cannot find another job. Many businesses that are at the precipice of bankruptcy will have to enter a merger or be absorbed by a larger business. In essence, all of 2008 will be all about business throughout the world, and a huge amount of paper money will have to be printed that will create more inflationary pressures. However, since Dr. Carl Johan Calleman's interpretation of the Mayan calendar's World Tree indicates a complete reversal between the eastern and western hemispheres, it becomes quite obvious why Asian businesses are booming and America is experiencing a rapid economic decline, which accommodates the karma-balancing, spiritual law of cause-and-effect regarding the excessive American consumerism of the past. Like it or not, America is getting what it deserves!

Competing with the optimism that Jupiter and Pluto in Sagittarius had been generating all during 2007, the opposition of Saturn (karma, duty, discipline, restrictions) and Neptune (the primary spiritual planet) was adversely affecting global stock markets and many material-oriented endeavors and activities, especially during the critical time period when the opposition was *exact* on February 28, 2007. Since astrologers call this pairing of planets the "Dreadful Duo", it can be understood why the rampaging stock market in Shanghai, China, plunged 9 percent on February 27, albeit the exact day of the opposition was on the 28th. Of course, the strong astrological influence really was enough, but it would appear that spiritual forces intervened to assure that the demise occurred during the potent-ending number of 27. The effect of this Chinese stock market plunge engendered a chain-reaction that quickly "circumnavigated" the globe, causing other stock markets to decline sharply also. As usual, and especially induced by the optimism of Sagittarius, the financial analysts quickly dissipated their fears, proclaimed an "overbought" condition that required a "correction" (take profits!), and proceded to resume the so-called bull—a fitting word—market. To fortify the effect of the number 9 during this 9 percent plunge, it was reported that this had been the worst brief decline in nine (cyclic number 9) years for the Shanghai stock exchange. Moreover, the accompanying astrological condition of Sun in Pisces, with its associated solar 12th house of self-undoing, certainly must have exacerbated the negative scenario, and also because money and spiritual Pisces are not compatible.

The Saros cycle of eighteen (time number 18) full years, regarding solar *eclipses*, that began in1989 (number 27 world year of big endings), may have been instrumental concerning the momentous dismantling of the depressing Berlin Wall and the initiation of the ending process of the Soviet Union. The student revolt at Tianamen Square in China, also in 1989, may have been a result of this same eclipse cycle. Empirically speaking, astrologers always are wary of eclipses, solar or lunar.

The next sequential Saros solar eclipse cycle was eighteen (18) full years later in 2007, so its effect was combined with another number 9 world year of endings, and this negative condition was aggravated further by the potent, rectifying influence of the Saturn-Neptune opposition. No wonder that the U.S. dollar really ended its long reign as global monetary king because of America's refusal to face the reality of the enormity of its financial quagmire.

Since the number 9 is the *cyclic* number for the affairs of humankind, as indicated by the 9-month gestation period for the creation of a physical human being, then the nine years from 1989 would be 1998, and, again, these four numerals would constitute another 27/9 world year of potent endings. Moreover, since 3 is the *whole* number and 3 x 666 = 1998 and the number 666 in the Book of Revelation pertains to *buying* and *selling* (Rev. 13:17), it becomes evident why a severe global financial crisis occurred in 1998. As cited in Chapter 3, it should be remembered that the annual tribute that King Solomon received was 666 talents of gold (I Kings 10:14-15), which has always been the standard for all paper currencies. Russia defaulted on its huge debt in 1998 and some Asian countries went bankrupt. A major

U.S. hedge fund, Long-Term Capital Management, collapsed. However, with the assistance of jovial, optimistic Sagittarius, the U.S. Federal Reserve quickly printed enough fiat money to "paper over" the crisis, and the financial tumor was stabilized temporarily, but now in 2008 it has resurged and metastasized into a seemingly incurable cancerous condition that can spread globally, especially concerning the daunting, pervasive nature of the *derivatives* structure.

Another financially-negative astrological scenario during 1998 involved the changing transit of the main spiritual planet, Neptune, as it entered the humanitarian sign of Aquarius. Perhaps the effect of this new astrological influence was what the Edgar Cayce spiritual source meant when it mentioned that a new type of energy would be activated for the world in 1998. When we again realize that 1998 was a 27/9 world year of big endings, this obviously was connected to the 40-year "testing period" (1958–1998) that the Cayce source had revealed long ago, and this in turn seems to have been connected to the number 666 in Revelation (3 x 666 = 1998). Hence, the financial manipulations and extreme preoccupation with material matters in 1998 could have induced a Neptune purging and cleansing effect, especially concerning the evolutionary process and spiritual destiny of humankind.

Having discussed and evaluated the financial and material conditions regarding the astrological meaning, purpose and effect of Neptune, its continuing transit of Aquarius should be producing another effect that is associated with its assigned ruler, Uranus. This is the planet associated with sudden changes and revolution, and the influence from the Neptune transit of Aquarius will continue until February of 2012, which is the predicted and calculated ending year for the Mayan Sacred Calendar/Tzolkin. Moreover, Uranus in still transiting the martyrdom sign of Pisces until early March of 2011, just when the annual transit of

Sun in Pisces occurs, magnifying this influence. One astrologer has called the 1998-2012 period the "purification phase" in the spiritual evolution of humankind, and this same period most likely is the time that Christ referred to as the "birth pangs of the new age." Obviously, all of humankind should anticipate an increase and expansion of deteriorating global conditions—think global warming—regarding all aspects of life on planet Earth, such as the depletion of virtually all natural resources that should drive their values/prices to prohibitive levels. A primary global concern that was discussed at a recent G8 summit meeting pertained to the looming specter of accelerating starvation, both as a consequence of high commodity prices and their dwindling availability. Indeed, everyone in the world should be trying to find some way to grow their food, and perhaps it is time to experiment with the pyramid power that Dr. G. Patrick Flanagan investigated and proved back in the early 1970s, and his data are contained in his book, Pyramid Power (1975).

A succinct reference and example of the influence of the spiritual science of numbers upon financial markets is when the Dow Jones Industrial Average (DJIA) suffered a 508.13-point loss on October 19, 1987, which was the worst one-day decline (up to that time) since the stock market collapse on October 29, 1929, which became the harbinger of the Great Depression. The reader by now probably has observed that this precise number collectively vibrates to the number 17 (5+0+8+1+3) of suffering, and the digits/numerals of the date (1+0+1+9+1+9+8+7) add to 36, which reduces and vibrates to the cyclic and ending number 9. Also, the numerals 3-6-9 comprise the most potent of the three triads (1-4-7, 2-5-8 and 3-6-9), and this strongest vibratory energy apparently is derived from the time number 18 that results from the combination of 3, 6 and 9. Referring to the "Black Tuesday" day in 1929, the numerals of the entire date (1+0+2+9+1+9+2+9) collectively vibrate to the number 33, which is the Christ Number and also the number of *responsibility* and *adjustments*, and the climactic scenario of this date manifested such a severe adjustment period that it continued until the end of World War II.

The worst or largest one-day point loss during the entire long history and activity of the DJIA occurred on September 17(!) in 2001, which was the first day that the stock markets had resumed trading following the traumatic destruction of the World Trade Towers in New York City by terrorists. This was the very same date (September 17, 2001) as for the calculated chronological ending time of the Great Pyramid in Egypt, whose primary numerical theme is the number 17 of suffering and redemption. (Late note added just prior to book publication: On September 17, 2008, America experienced perhaps its worst catastrophic financial crisis in its history, which was precipitated by the collapse of the nebulous, risky trading instruments classified as "derivatives", which are really only ridiculous, unscrupulous bets and debts.).

To compound the effects of this number 17 day, the DJIA closed the day with a shocking 684.81-point loss, and this precise number collectively vibrates to the number 27 of dramatic endings.

Since monetary interest rates are such an integral component of the trading activity on Wall Street, it was quite notable that the U.S. Federal Reserve raised interest rates seventeen (17) *consecutive* times during the two-year period that extended into 2006, which was a very materialistic number 8 world year. Seemingly oblivious to this normally-suppressing action, the DJIA closed at an all-time high on December 27, 2006, just as the number 8 very materialistic world year must have induced, and the number 27 provided the climactic ending of the old DJIA record. Astrologically, Sun in Capricorn (big business and all material concerns) supplied accompanying strong planetary energy, just as it always does during the annual Christmas holidays, which should make the Christ Spirit quite uncomfortable. Actually,

156

the "traditional" Christmas stock market rally is a continuation of the "traditional" American Thanksgiving rally that always is precipitated by the unbridled optimism of Sun in Sagittarius at that time, and this latter rally always begins following the typical late October decline in the value of stocks because of the *death* and *rebirth* influence of Sun in Scorpio.

To put this financial "chain-reaction" scenario for stock markets during the last quarter of almost any year into perspective, the annual transit of Sun in Libra (22 Sept.–23 Oct.) manifests a strong emphasis pertaining to *balance*. The previous discussion of the severe decline (worst since 1929) of the New York stock exchanges on October 19, 1987, is a good example. Instead of waiting for the typical Scorpio effect of purging grossly-unbalanced markets in late October, a *rebalancing* occurred near the ending of the Libra influence and effect. The immediately subsequent normal Scorpio effect from its associated 8th (very material number) solar house of *death* and *rebirth* was most notable on the disastrous date of October 29, 1929. Indeed, statistical research has revealed that the most precarious *average* day in the long history of the NYSE is October 27, which appears to be an accurate analysis based on the numerological meaning of this number of big endings. Since the zodiacal sign of Scorpio is also associated with *regeneration*, then the best time to buy the depressed stocks—the word "securities" should never be used—should be after the middle of November. An initial rally by impatient traders (the general public is still in shock at this time) usually begins earlier, but this generally is a false start wherein the most aggressive traders impatiently sell to generate at least a small profit, which certainly delights the tax collectors. The Scorpio period for rebirth ends about the 22nd of November, and this is immediately followed by the very optimistic Sagittarius influence that lasts until December 21 at the winter solstice. Then the extremely materialistic Capricorn period that influences businesses at all levels and stimulates the greed aspect of human nature begins, and this astrological influence continues until about the 19th of January, when Aquarian energy begins.

Since the best time to purchase stocks based only on astrology is being discussed, there is one other period in the summer that usually should be successful (omitting 2008 for its credit crisis). Sun in Leo from July 22nd to August 22nd involves the activation of the solar 5th house that pertains to creativity, speculation, entertainment and even romance, which explains why so many "investors" tend to "fall in love" with certain stocks at this time. This combination of Leo traits results in the "traditional" summer rally that generally continues throughout the serious work and analytical influence of Virgo (August 22 to September 22), and even throughout the balancing influence of Libra (October 19, 1987, was a rare exception that precluded the assigned duties of Scorpio, perhaps because the markets were so far out of balance that a corrective action was mandatory concerning the law of cause and effect). Historically, the Leo effect depresses the price of gold and silver each August.

Contrarily, perhaps the worst time (at least astrologically) to purchase stocks or invest in anything is the period from February 19 to March 20 in any year because the influence from Sun in Pisces is not conducive to monetary and business endeavors or speculation. The associated solar 12th house is basically spiritually-oriented and pertains to compassion, tolerance and self-doing, possibly even to the ultimate degree of martyrdom. Since this Piscean influence applies to all of the activities of humankind, perhaps the best example of the misuse of this vibrational energy is the immoral attack on and invasion of Iraq on March 19, 2003 (date vibrates to 18), while the Pisces influence and effect still was functioning, which virtually assured that the best results possible would be merely a Pyrrhic victory with prohibitive costs. This is an appropriate example for this chapter concerning economics because the staggering financial costs—boxes of one-hundred dollar bills even disappeared!—of this war actually have administered the coup de grace to America's economic structure and stability that the balance sheets of any *private* business would reveal as a state of bankruptcy. Of course, they cannot "cook the books" by quickly printing billions of fiat dollars as the U.S. Federal Reserve can do. Note: Terrorist Osama Bin Laden's stated basic plan is to destroy America financially, and the naïve Bush *Regime* has fallen blindly into his trap by initiating a war in Iraq instead of pursuing him in Afghanistan immediately following his dramatic destruction of the financial center in New York.

Another interesting and supportive illustration of the influence of numbers on economics and business involved the merger (takeover) of U.S. automaker, Chrysler, with German automaker, Daimler, that lasted for nine (9 is the number of endings) years. As reported in the media, in May of 2007 (a number 9 world year of endings), Daimler disposed of its obviously unprofitable Chryler acquisition by paying $675 (= 18/9) million to a private-equity firm to cover the medical expenses of many retirees to whom it owed $18 (= 9) billion. Daimler had paid $36 (9) billion for Chrysler obviously in 1998, which was a 27/9 world year of big endings, and especially for large automaker Chrysler.An awareness and understanding of numerological—and most likely astrological also—factors obviously could have saved Daimler a huge amount of money and misery. Many years of empirical astrological information strongly indicate that any business entity should have its natal horoscope evaluated before making any serious business plans or initiating any major action(s).

In the early part of the twentieth century, Russian economist Nikolai Kondratieff studied the economic history of the world's supreme capitalist country (at that time), the

159

United States of America, reportedly in response to dictator Joseph Stalin's demand. His thorough analysis resulted in his world-renowned Economic Long Wave that encompasses the entire economic history of America. The acknowledged present expert analyst and interpreter of the Economic Long Wave is Ian Gordon in Vancouver, B.C., Canada, who daily monitors the Wave (as displayed on the global Internet) so as to provide the best possible investing advice to his clients.

To graphically depict the correlation of combined numerological and astrological influences on the economy of the U.S.A. (these vibrational energies should apply to the entire world), this author has added four vertical lines at evenly-spaced horizontal locations on the Economic Long Wave (see Figure 5) that correspond to the entire 230-year period from 1790 to 2020 that obviously includes the immediate future. Each vertical straight line indicates a point in time when the spiritual planet, Neptune, entered a zodiacal *earth* sign of which there are only three in the zodiac. Since Neptune is classified as the outer planet that is associated with spiritual consciousness, it becomes quite uncomfortable in its role as a living cosmological entity whenever it transits a materialistic earth sign (Taurus, Virgo and Capricorn in proper sequential order), which occurs every 54 (9) *full* earth years because its solar orbit encompasses 164.79 (= 27/9) earth years to complete. It should be noted on the chart that Neptune entered the three earth signs at different points in time on the four Autumn periods as shown. The reason that the Taurus and Virgo time lines indicate an accelerated Winter period is most likely attributed to the association of Taurus with the solar 2nd house of *money* and financial institutions, whereas Virgo is associated with the solar 6th house of *work* and *health*. Hence, we can see why in 1929 a severe depression began that resulted in millions of workers becoming unemployed, but their health survived because at that time much of the U.S. populace resided on farms, which is ominous and foreboding regarding the present opposite condition of the masses in cities. The similar short Autumn period for Taurus probably was induced by a tight money supply and credit condition, which had been a typical financial problem during the lengthy economic recovery from the chaos and monetary costs of the U.S. Civil War.

Concerning the much longer Autumn periods for the two Neptune transits of the big business sign of Capricorn, this zodiacal sign is associated with the solar 10th house of career, reputation, prestige, and is the primary business sign that also involves world governments and their leaders. Hence, we can see here that large businesses and corporations would have possessed the money and aggressiveness to perpetuate the boom cycle in complete defiance of the spiritual influence of Neptune. Again, the human birthright of *free will* can, and obviously did, transcend and supersede any amount of spiritual energy, and this is especially notable on this chart because both transits of Neptune began right at the beginning of both of the Autumn periods concerning Capricorn. As a result of these two *extended* Autumn periods of time, the Winter period for at least the first Capricorn cycle was a sharper decline as necessitated by the 54-year cyclic time factor. Of course, the current second Capricorn period is incomplete. Prior to this author's alteration of the broken or hyphenated Winter line, the previous or original slope line was less severe, and the projected anticipated bottoming year had been 2020. However, based on current U.S. economic conditions and the scenario that was predicted in the dire prophecy of the Fatima spiritual source and the interpretations of both Drs Carl Johan Calleman (Mayan Sacred Calendar) and James J. Hurtak (The Keys of Enoch), the concluding year of 2010 appears to be more realistic, especially when the idealized Kondratieff pattern is compared to the actual, seemingly out of control, U.S. economic activity curve at the top of the graph.

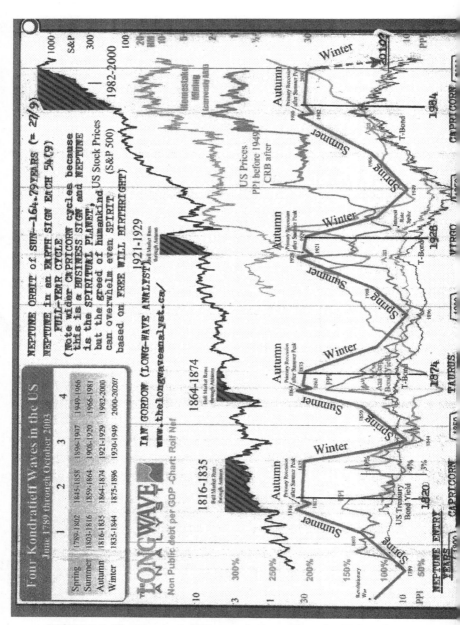

FIGURE 5: The Kondratieff Economic Long Wave for U.S.A. Economy

Whereas the 1928 entry of Neptune in the work and health sign of Virgo apparently was involved with the mass unemployment of the Great Depression, the present transit and astrological influence of Saturn (destiny, duty, discipline and penalties or rewards, depending on the karmic polarity) in Virgo (September, 2007 to September, 2010, including retrograde periods) indicates that unemployment and health conditions will be an increasing problem, and the AIDS pandemic may be greatly exacerbated. However, regarding the *rewards* side of the Saturn-Virgo equation, it is possible that a spiritually-qualified medical researcher will provide an international solution to this global scourge. Of course, it may be replaced with an even worse health nightmare, as the Book of Revelation in the Holy Bible depicts. This Saturn-in-Virgo astrological scenario also indicates that the next elected American president who takes office on January 20, 2009, will be strongly influenced to try to solve —not just mitigate—the national health insurance problem and other medical inadequacies, but there is virtually no money available without printing much more, thereby inducing even higher inflationary pressures. The classic Catch-22 scenario continues. The supreme ego of presumed president Barrick Obama most likely will be tested, and public disappointment concerning failure may greatly deflate this ego. His mellifluous campaign rhetoric would be forgotten and his lofty promises may become unfulfilled if all of the negative astrological indicators and prophetic sources prove to be accurate. As Christ said (Matthew 24), it will be a time like no other in the history of the world!

Again regarding the work and health aspects of Saturn in Virgo, alternative/complementary medical modalities should proliferate and prosper because they will be far less expensive than the costs of conventional medicine, and people will be urged to become responsible for their own health, especially concerning proper nutrition. Many people finally will begin to try to grow some fruits and vegetables. Nutrition is a normal component of Virgo, and scientific research will expand even further with its study of the complete nutritional values of all available foods in the world, and the U.S. government's Food Pyramid may have to be revised again. Moreover, since the Kirlian electrical photography reveals that the pyramid configuration apparently is an efficient focusing device for the subatomic, metaphysical *ether* (see Chapter 4), perhaps people could be induced to utilize small pyramids (type of material seems to be irrelevant) to enhance the quality of foods, as well as preserve them, or at least to extend their longevity regarding safe consumption, just as Dr. G. Patrick Flanagan had proposed in the early 1970s. Additionally, perhaps the full value of *xenon* concerning all aspects of life—not just medical—will be discovered, even concerning the raising of human *consciousness*.

CHAPTER 10

The Relevance and Integration of Extraterrestrial and Cosmic Numbers

To begin with our closest relative and natural satellite, our single Moon, it orbits Earth every 27 *full* days in reference to the stars and it turns on its axis only once every 27 full days, so this apparently very important *double* triplication of the human destiny number 9 is obviously still in effect beyond its mother planet, Earth. Its diameter at the equator is 2160 miles, which again vibrates to the critical number 9 (2+1+6+0). We may ask why Earth only has one moon when even tiny asteroid 87 Sylvia has *two* moons named Romulus and Remus. Earth's lone moon has a tremendous effect on Earth's oceans and arguably on the very emotions of human beings, especially those who have prominent astrological water signs (Cancer, Scorpio and Pisces, sequentially) or who have numerous planets in these water signs, as denoted in the natal horoscope. According to astronomers, our special moon's distance from Earth has changed appreciably during past millennia, but from a spiritual perspective it obviously is at the correct distance from Earth at this time so as to manifest the required gravitational influence on all of humankind at this critical period concerning our spiritual evolutionary process, and especially regarding emotional stability during our personal interactions. The presence and influence of more than one moon would alter drastically the Divine Plan for all souls in embodiment in the earth plane during each sojourn that may be karmically required for the process of Perfection. Besides the gravitational energy aspect from the moon, its illumination by the sun determines the amount of reflected light that will bathe all human beings and other denizens of Earth, and each full-moon phase distributes the most vibrational electromagnetic light energy that logically must have an effect on the natural

165

electrical and electrochemical processes in all cellular physical bodies. Excessive erratic or aberrational human emotional activity and behavior during each full-moon phase was noted by psychiatrists long ago, and this apparently motivated observers to invent the words *lunatic* and *lunacy* to accommodate these emotional conditions.

New lunar observations from NASA's Spitzer Space Telescope suggest that moons like that of Earth's are uncommon in at least our local universe. From a numerological perspective, it is somewhat interesting that during the momentous year of 1998 (= 27/9 and 3 x 666) traces of water ice were detected and discovered in some craters at the poles of our special satellite.

Astronomer Johannes Kepler was reported to have philosophized, "Astrology is astronomy brought down to Earth to affect the affairs of man." The spiritual science of astrology utilizes the phases of the Moon (which they always capitalize), and especially lunar *eclipses*, to determine the emotional condition of an entity at any specific time. To concur with Kepler's assessment and hypothesis, the Edgar Cayce spiritual source strongly urged *everyone* to study and apply astrology in connection with the decisions, direction and activities in their life, while cautioning the proper interpretation and application of astrological influences. In other words, people should not become "lost in the stars", and especially not to become "astrological hypochondriacs."

Since the spiritual science of astrology specifies that the three (whole number 3) outer planets, Uranus, Neptune and Pluto (sequentially), are instrumental concerning human consciousness and soul development, then any knowledge and awareness of any numerological correspondence should be beneficial to the spiritual truth seeker. The numbers associated with these three planets reveal the omnipotence, omniscience and omnipresence

166

of Creative Forces/God or a Divine Being who has a Master Plan for humankind, and these planets may be considered as "living cosmological entities."

Regarding proximity to Earth, Uranus is the first of the three outer planets that, astrologically, pertains to *change* (often surprise changes, either negative or positive) and also pertains to electricity and revolution of any kind. It also involves inventions, new methods, ideas and reforms. It was discovered in 1781, which was a number 17 world year, thus indicating that the timing for this "discovery" definitely was not accidental, and it indicated that it was now time for humankind to begin a new phase of experience with the suffering and redemption traits of the number 17. The inclusion of this additional planet in the repertoire of the spiritual science of astrology also meant that astrologers would have to start observing the relationship between the activities of human beings and the corresponding location of Uranus at the same time, as well as its position as related to our Sun and the other planets so as to assign the correct types of influences that Uranus was applying to human desires and activities. Since the time factor regarding the solar orbit of distant Uranus is so long, as well as its complete transit through all twelve signs of the zodiac, the relatively-short, 227-year period since 1781 must have required strong intuitive forces for astrologers to have obtained all the present characteristics that have been assigned to Uranus, but these influences appear to be quite accurate.

Uranus has 27 moons (as of 2007), which again is the triplication of the destiny number 9. Uranus rotates on a very unusual 98-(=17) degree axis and has a rotational period (day) of 17 full hours. As mentioned previously in this book, the number 98 contains the two most important numerals concerning the destiny and spiritual evolutionary process for our Adamic race of human beings. Whereas the number 9 is the very specific human destiny number vibration, the number 8 pertains to the material earth plane, and the soul only can be perfected via its processing through three-dimensional atomic matter, thus producing the number 17! Uranus can induce a revolution in anyone's life, depending on its astrological position in the current horoscope, and especially during the period from early 2003 until early 2011 because Uranus is now transiting the compassionate, humanitarian, martyrdom sign of Pisces. Hence, the most surprise change(s) should be in the life of any entity who has Sun in Pisces (solar 1st house of new beginnings) and those persons who have prominent planets in the zodiacal sign of Pisces in their natal horoscope. Since this period ends immediately following the beginning of the 9th and last Universal Creation Cycle of the Mayan Sacred Calendar/Tzolkin in early February, 2011, the present Uranus transit and activation of Pisces obviously is intended by Spirit to induce as many human beings as possible (dependent upon personal desires and the free-will birthright) to become humanitarians and to "sacrifice" the ego and consider others before Self. The solar 12th house of sacrifice and self-denial that is associated with Pisces is really the domain of the soul and its superconscious mind that only those who have been assigned the basic Pisces character truly can understand completely, and corroborating examples would be Edgar Cayce, Albert Schweitzer, Albert Einstein, Rudolf Steiner and Hugh Lynn Cayce. Hence, this should assure that the individual will qualify to experience the illumination and enlightenment that pertain to the 9th Universal Creation Cycle from February 11, 2011 until October 28, 2011, which is an approximate 9-month period that is similar to the gestation period for creating a physical human being. (Incidentally, it should be noted that the latter Cayce, who was the son of trance medium Edgar Cayce, conceived and built the world-renowned Association for Research and Enlightenment as the primary integral component of the Edgar Cayce Foundation, and his Pisces character, coupled with his ultimate 27/9 Life Path/Lesson, must have contributed considerably to his huge accomplishment that now attracts scientists, theologians, philosophers, and all types of medical doctors and Light seekers from around the world.)

Neptune, which is known astrologically as the primary *spiritual* planet or cosmological living entity, has an orbital period of 164.79 (= 27/9) Earth years and rotates every 16.11 (= 9) hours (day). Its temperature is -261 (= 9) degrees Fahrenheit (the modern Celsius scale has not been evaluated for these statistics and values). As noted in Chapter 9, this spiritual planet has a very significant impact on global economics whenever it transits and influences all three (whole number) of the zodiacal earth signs of Taurus, Virgo and Capricorn. As mentioned previously, spiritual Neptune entered the New Age sign of Aquarius in the extremely critical year of 1998 (3 x 666 = 1998 and 1+9+9+8= 27, the triplication of the destiny number 9), and it will continue in this very revolutionary sign until early in the final critical year of 2012, according to the interpreted prophecy of the Mayan Sacred Calendar/Tzolkin. This approximately 14-year period has been called the "Purification Phase" concerning the spiritual evolutionary process for humankind, and the accompanying Uranus-in-Pisces factor and effect will manifest a revolution and transformation in human Consciousness.

Pluto is the planet (officially demoted to "dwarf" planet status in 2006 by spiritually-ignorant astronomers) and "living cosmological entity" that should be of most interest at this crucial time in the predestined spiritual evolution of humankind as the special Adamic race that the Christ Soul had initiated. Whereas astrologers have assigned the word, *transformation*, to Pluto's spiritual purpose, the Edgar Cayce spiritual source said that Pluto pertains to *consciousness* and that its influence is *increasing* (!), but this assessment probably was announced during one of the two lengthy periods when Pluto's long, elliptical orbit placed it *inside* the orbit of Neptune. Hence, this closer proximity to Earth twice during its 247.9-Earth-year orbit of the sun obviously would give Pluto a stronger influence on human beings. From a philosophical perspective, the words "transformation" and "consciousness" essentially are interchangeable because one begets the other. The fact that Pluto was not "discovered" until February 18 (time number) in 1930 appears to indicate that humankind was destined to begin an awareness of the influence of Pluto in all its daily activities and affairs. The diminutive size of Pluto suggests that its influence normally would be relatively subtle, except when it is positioned closer to Earth than Neptune. Further emphasizing the *time* factor regarding the 18th day of February, Pluto's inclination of orbit to ecliptic is 17.1 degrees, and 18 vibrates to 9 (cyclic number), as does 1+7+1, and the number 17 and its number 1 decimal equal 18, which accommodates both of these critical numbers.

Regarding again the important spiritual science of astrology, it follows that astrologers were quick to incorporate even tiny Pluto into their planetary repertoire and to begin observing and evaluating its possible influence on human beings. Even now, they still are learning and assimilating the full spiritual meaning and purpose for this tiny sphere of intended influence, but they (logically) seem to be expanding the purpose and scope of astrology too far by incorporating *asteroids* into the philosophical system that appears to be sufficient with the assimilation of Pluto. When astronomers named Pluto after the Roman god of the Underworld, this obviously must have engendered some confusion concerning its exact spiritual mission for humankind, so Pluto was designated as the ruler of the zodiacal sign of Scorpio because this sign is associated with the solar 8th house of *death* and *rebirth*. Scorpio has a strong affinity with *regeneration* of all types, but especially concerning the cellular physical anatomy of human beings.

Astronomer Clyde Tombaugh was searching for his so-called Planet X when he most likely was guided by Spirit to find tiny Pluto, which is surprising because Pluto orbits our star, Sun, at a very odd 17 (!) degrees in relation to all the other eight planets whose solar orbits are essentially in one plane. It should not require an excessive stretch of the reader's imagination as to the spiritual purpose that obviously was intended concerning the supreme importance of this 17-degree aberrational, oblique orbital path of the ninth (9!) and last planet in our solar system. At present, astronomers are debating and arguing about the total quantity of planets in our solar system, not realizing that an exclusion of Pluto would reduce the quantity to the very materialistic number 8, thereby thwarting the purpose of the human destiny number 9. Hence, our solar system would be unable to function as a spiritual system, realm and collective dimension—there are 8 dimensions in our solar system, according to the Edgar Cayce spiritual source—without a ninth (9) culminating sphere of influence (Pluto). Indeed, the Pluto effect is positively essential for the completion of the spiritual evolutionary process of humankind, as profoundly indicated by its revealing 17-degree orbital position (think of the 17th day of both months concerning the start of the Great Flood and grounding of Noah's ark).

Since the Edgar Cayce spiritual source stated long ago that the "testing period" for humankind would be during the 40- (strong biblical testing number) year time period between 1958 and 1998, it appears quite relevant that the last time Pluto was *inside* (closer to Earth) the orbit of Neptune was during the period 1979 to 1998. Based on all the other references in this book to this "destiny" year of 1998, and especially to the fact that this number is a product of 3 x 666(!), the ending year for this closer Pluto position relative to Earth tends to reinforce and corroborate the spiritual role of Pluto in the affairs and consciousness of humankind. In his book, 1998: Year of

Destiny, the late metaphysician, Raymond Ouellette, presented other sources of information and data concerning the paramount importance of this year for humankind, especially regarding the chronology of the Great Pyramid in Egypt. However, since the revered, tested Cayce spiritual source called the 40-year period from 1958 to 1998 the "testing period" for humankind, meticulous, metaphysical investigator, Raymond Ouellette, logically presumed (just as this author had done) that in the concluding year of 1998 all human beings would be given a "final exam" concerning their spiritual evolutionary progress and the status of their karmic debts. Moreover, Pluto reached its perihelion (closest to Sun) in 1989, and both 1989 and 1998 were 27/9 world years of dramatic and memorable endings that are depicted in other chapters of this book. As mentioned above, even spiritual planet, Neptune, was involved in the pivotal year of 1998 when it began its transit and activation of Aquarius (sign of *revolution* and the New Age) that will continue until the next destiny year of 2012 that is indicated from the Mayan calendar.

Albeit the three consciousness outer planets are the primary concern of this chapter, perhaps the activity of "taskmaster" Saturn (the karma and destiny planet) should be noted and examined concerning its relevance to the general astrological scenario for these ending years and days of the Piscean Age. As mentioned in Chapter 9, Saturn is presently activating the work and health zodiacal sign of Virgo until September 21, 2010, at which time it will enter the *balance* and *partnerships* sign of Libra. Everyone will be tested regarding their ability to maintain balance while interacting with others, especially concerning their marriage partner and also all legally-nonbinding partnerships, which should be extremely difficult during these "birth pang" (per Christ in Matthew 24) years preceding the New Age. Saturn will then enter the death and rebirth sign of Scorpio (regeneration) on October 5, 2012, while Sun in Libra continues until October 23, 2012. The Scorpio effect will begin only eleven weeks prior to the critical ending date of December 21, 2012, as indicated by the Mayan Long Count, as interpreted by numerous investigators and interpreters. Saturn (discipline, duty, karma, destiny and rewards) in Scorpio (death and rebirth) at that time appears to mean that all those entities who had experienced and passed the spiritual requirements of the ninth (9) and final Universal Creation Cycle during its 9-month period in 2011 should now (late 2012) qualify for an electro-chemical and photonic transformation from three-dimensional, physical beings to fifth-dimensional *whole Light beings*! Of course, humans will transcend the *fourth* dimension that relates to *time*.

Moving closer to Earth and our red (color of anger) masculine neighbor, Mars, a NASA spacecraft that was very appropriately named Mariner 9 (!) sent back startling photographs in 1972 (number 1 world year of new beginnings) that depicted groups of massive pyramidal and tetrahedral structures. These structures are positioned intelligently in grid patterns with units of 18 (time number) structures. Whereas NASA scientists apparently are at a loss to explain this mystery and obviously determined to shrug it off as merely a natural anomaly, the intensely-metaphysical Book of Knowledge: The Keys of Enoch reveals that these coherent structural patterns have an intelligent relationship with Saturn, which is the planet entity that is associated with the immutable spiritual law of cause-and-effect (defined simply as karma). Referred to as *maser* (microwave amplification by stimulated emission of radiation) grids, the unit of 18 structures has 9 (!) "A-line controls" and also 9 "B-line controls" that are connected with a "non-planetary pyramid-5 formation" , which is the central model for information processing. This is extremely complex for a three-dimensional human being to comprehend and assimilate, but the recipient of this esoteric, *future science* information, Dr. James J. Hurtak, certainly understands the concept, meaning and purpose of this phenomenon as it pertains to the spiritual evolution of humankind. His Academy for Future Science in Ava, Missouri, should be contacted regarding an elucidation of present and developing cosmic conditions, especially as they now are, and will be, affecting the spiritual destiny of humankind. Perhaps when humankind has reached the Mayan calendar's conclusive, terminating year of 2012 (or even before during the scenario of enlightenment and brotherly love in 2011) we will have assimilated the full meaning and purpose of the Martian mystery. Alternatively, it may not become part of our awareness until humankind has been apprised of the results of the planned Mars probing mission that has been scheduled to leave Earth in October, 2011 (ending month of the last and ninth Mayan Creation Cycle) and should arrive at Mars in April, 2012. However, if Dr. Carl Johan Calleman's spiritual scenario for the year 2011 is correct, then it most likely will preclude the planned Mars mission.

As of mid-2008, some 2012-oriented persons have been speculating regarding the cosmic event that they maintain will occur in 2012 in which there will be an alignment of Earth's Sun with the galactic center of our Milky Way Galaxy. This developing cosmic condition may be an integral component of the mind-boggling, comprehensive universal scenario that is described in The Book of Knowledge that is cited above, and especially its depiction of an "electromagnetic null zone."

Concerning all of the nine (9) planets in our solar system and their individual orbits, the general consensus is that the "all-planet synod" (all planets aligned on one side of the sun) occurs every 180 years, which vibrates to the time number 18 with a magnifier and that appears to be numerologically logical. However, a more precise measured time factor reveals that the all-planet synod actually occurs slightly sooner at 179 *full* years, and these numerals collectively vibrate to the number 17!

If we fix our nocturnal gaze 37 light years beyond Earth, we can perceive the brightest star Arcturus (or *archturus* in The Book of Knowledge: The Keys of Enoch), which is in the constellation of Bootes (the herdsman). This cosmic giant of a fixed star is actually very important to humankind because the Edgar Cayce spiritual source revealed that when *souls* complete their mandatory perfective process in the three-dimensional earth plane of matter, they are directed to Arcturus for further processing. This obviously is the domain that Roman Catholicism refers to as "purgatory", albeit this seems to be an appropriate label for the life process in Schoolhouse Earth. To corroborate, substantiate and validate the Cayce spiritual source, the Book of Knowledge: The Keys of Enoch, refers to *Archturus* (the *h* is added to incorporate the h-bar constant) as a "Mid-Way station" concerning soul-processing and "soul-mapping" that is associated with the herdsman aspect of Arc(h)turus. Additionally, it states that Archturus is the "first threshold of clearance for travel beyond our consciousness time zone." Moreover, it says that there are certain pyramids in South America (Peru?) that are in direct alignment with Archturus and which give the timetable of astrophysical and geophysical change! Broadly, Archturus should figure prominently in the imminent next phase of the predestined spiritual evolutionary process of all souls (2012?).

In perfect accordance with the destiny number 9 for humankind, the Book of Knowledge: Keys of Enoch refers to the "Council of Nine", who are a "Tribunal of Teachers" who govern our immediate galactic region (Milky Way Galaxy). Since our solar system is positioned near the edge of this galaxy, this makes it possible for humans on Earth to view it so easily from this peripheral location.

Supporting the "Spiral Galaxy Theory" of astronomers, they have identified nine (9!) bands of stars and gas in the Milky Way Galaxy. The Book of Knowledge also refers to nine (9!)

dimensions in our local universe and further states that the "ninth [9] spatial wave" controls gravitational lines of force. Regarding the number 9 and its relationship to "gravitational lines of force", this information correlates precisely with the profound statement that was made by the extraterrestrial being (see last paragraph of Chapter 4) that concerned the method of construction (levitation/anti-gravity) of the Great Pyramid in Egypt, and the Cayce spiritual source said the same regarding its construction from 10,490 to 10,390 B.C. Regarding the tremendous advantage of applying levitational forces, it seems implausible that it required 100 years to build the Pyramid, but the Cayce psychic information seemed to indicate that personal and/or political problems concerning a queen obviously induced negative, impeding factors that may have caused long construction delays. Concerning the nine (9) dimensions of our local *universe*, this also correlates with the Cayce information where it stated that there are eight (8) dimensions in our solar system, and the added dimension for our local universe may function as an encompassing, unifying, fortifying and completing dimension, just as the "vibrational energy" of the number 9 would indicate.

The primary theme of The Book of Knowledge: The Keys of Enoch involves 64 Keys of Enoch. The number 10 vibration for numerals 6 and 4 appear not to be in compliance and harmony with the number 9 theme and basis of this book. However, Dr. Hurtak was informed by spiritual sources that the first fifty-four (5 + 4 = 9) Keys apply to all aspects of all sciences that involve humankind, but the last ten (10 is the destiny number for the perfected soul, whereas 9 pertains merely to the *process* required to accomplish soul Perfection) Keys refer to the Ten Commandments that were presented to Moses on Mt. Sinai/ Horeb. The reason for including the number 64 at this point in this book is to offer validation of the contents of Dr. Hurtak's profound book and also the foundation of the Mayan Sacred Calendar/Tzolkin.

One of the primary authorities concerning the Mayan calendar is John Major Jenkins, who published his first book, Journey to the Mayan Underworld, in 1989, which was a very notable and important 27/9 world year of big endings (end of Berlin Wall and Soviet domination of Europe). His succeeding book, Maya Cosmogenesis 2012, was published in 1998, which was the second of this unusual pair of crucial 27/9 world years of big endings, and that also involved an intervening 9-year cycle. Mr. Jenkins discovered that the number 64 regarding the Mayan Sacred Calendar/Tzolkin was so basic that he wrote: "The PHI64 system is at the core of the Mayan calendar and Maya time philosophy in general." He also referred to their philosophy as "Maya Sacred Science."

Mayan researcher José Argüelles also cited the importance of the number 64 in his provocative 1987 (Harmonic Convergence year) book, The Mayan Factor: Path Beyond Technology, wherein he focuses on the 64 central units of the Tzolkin. He discovered that inscribed in this 64-unit matrix is the "code and game plan of human destiny, the path beyond technology." This corresponds with the comprehensive and full meaning of the 64 Keys of Enoch that were divinely imparted to Dr. James J. Hurtak in January, 1973, and later published in his 1977 book, The Book of Knowledge: The Keys of Enoch. (Note: It should be remembered that all of this complex information and true knowledge most likely originated from the Christ Soul in human embodiment as Amelius in Atlantis, as the Edgar Cayce spiritual source had derived and indicated from the divine Akashic Records or Book of Life.)

Dr. Argüelles has great hope for humankind and states that the final five-(number of man)year period from A.D. 2007–2012 will be "singularly directed to the emplacement of galactic synchronization crews at all the planetary light-body grid-nodes." This cosmological manifestation and transformation corresponds with the full magnitude of the universal scenario that is profoundly depicted in The Book of Knowledge: The Keys of Enoch.

Since the numeral 3 is the *whole* number, as validated by the Holy Trinity, a third example of the importance of the number 64 should be presented and discussed. Perhaps the ancient Chinese system of cosmology and philosophy, the I Ching, will serve to satisfy this requirement and wholeness, especially since there appears to be an increasing interest and application of this system concerning divination. As material and religious (involving much ignorance and form) pressures increase for the six billion-plus people in the world, the consequential stress is virtually coercing them to search for any source that may provide answers to their problems. The 64 hexagrams of the I Ching appear to accommodate every aspect of human desires, emotional traits and personal relationships. Alas, as this book strongly indicates, the *real* unifying synthesis of all aspects of life is the Christ, and He advised all of humankind to "Come to me and I will give you rest." Indeed, in these "last days" of the Piscean Age, every human entity should be focused on the Christ (as He advised), but the constant, seemingly-innumerable distractions of the global society make this task nearly impossible.

Perhaps this is beyond the scope of this book, but the numbers involved seem to justify this inclusion because of their relevance to the paramount, essential number 9 and its connection to the spiritual evolutionary process of humankind. In The Book of Knowledge: The Keys of Enoch, there is a reference to the triplicated number "6-6-6" versus the triplicated number "9-9-9." The reference is to the ninth (9!) Key of Enoch and its inversion, which is 6-6-6, the mysterious number in the Book of Revelation in the Holy Bible. There is reference to the "stellar programs of 9-9-9" or the "three-fold causality of Father-Son-Shekinah [Holy Spirit] universes operating together

178

on all nine [9] time cells of material creation, neutralizing the 6-6-6." This corresponds well with the basic meaning of the number 6 (*responsibility* and *adjustments*) in the very important spiritual science of numerology. Moreover, this "6-6-6" may have a relevance and parallel with the obviously very important number 666 in the Book of Revelation and its significance as the last of the 27(!) canonical books of the New Testament of the Holy Bible.

It would appear that this *universal* triplication (9-9-9) of the critical number 9 by the First Cause/Creative Forces/ God is the supreme emphasis and importance of the number 9 concerning the affairs and Destiny of humankind!

Made in the USA
Lexington, KY
10 December 2009